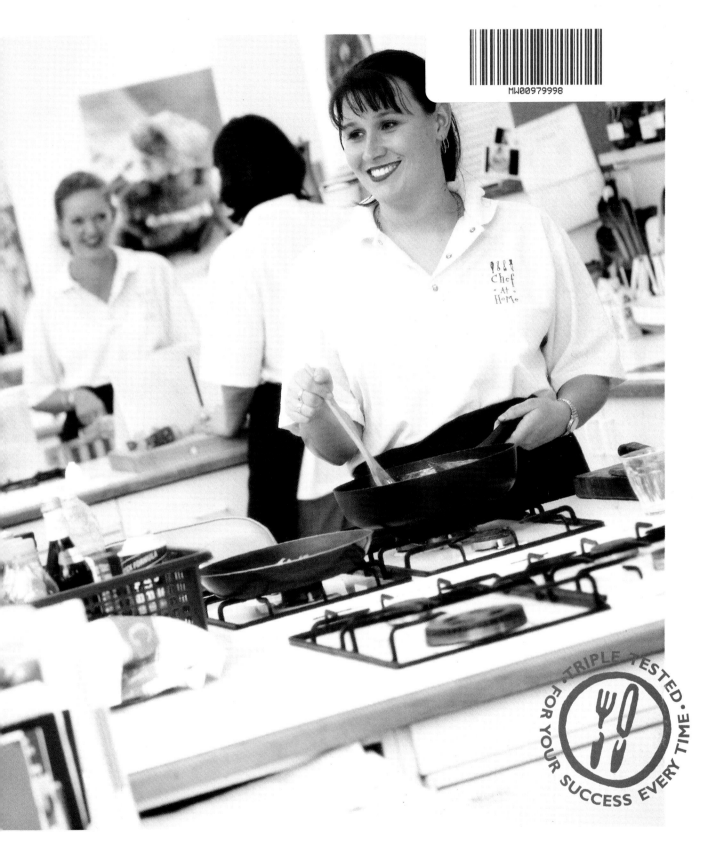

TRIPLE TESTED · FOR YOUR SUCCESS EVERY TIME

Although this book's called *Fantastic Cakes*, we could just as easily have named it "Fantasy Cakes", because that's what it is – a clever concoction full of the stuff of which legends are made. And you'll become a legend yourself when you reveal one of these fanciful creations to a rapt audience at the next family special occasion or for your child's birthday party. The absolutely fabulous cakes in this book may look extraordinary but, rest assured, you'll find them easy to make. Just be prepared to handle the compliments!

Pamela Clark

FOOD EDITOR

Contents

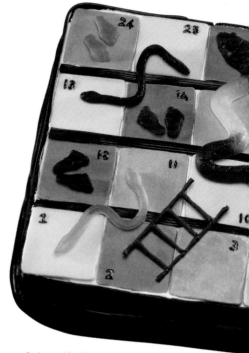

Snakes and Ladders, *page 6*

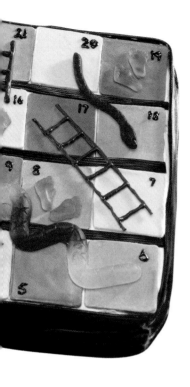

Balloon Bouquet, *page 10*

FOR THE CAKE:

3 x 340g packets buttercake mix

35cm x 45cm rectangular
   prepared board [page 115]

1 quantity Frosting [page 116]

green colouring

TO DECORATE, YOU WILL NEED:

8 square after-dinner mints

3 x 125g boxes chocolate
   mint sticks

3 x 200g packets spearmint leaves

Tic Tacs

thin red licorice rope

Grease 26cm x 36cm baking dish (base measurements), line base with baking paper. Using 3 packets, prepare cake mix according to directions; pour into prepared dish. Bake in a moderate oven for about 1 hour. Stand cake in dish 5 minutes; turn onto wire rack to cool.

1 Using paper pattern, cut out Stella Stegosaur's shape.

2 Place cake on board. Tint Frosting with green colouring; spread top and side of cake with Frosting.

3 Trim all sides of 1 after-dinner mint; using paper pattern as a guide, position this mint in centre of backbone. Trim and position remaining mints, decreasing in size slightly as they near the head and tail. Cut mints in half diagonally and fit to cake body so that they can be raised along the cut diagonal to look like armour-plated spikes.

4 Cut mint sticks in graduated lengths; place in position along back so that they support spikes, raising each in the centre.

5 Starting at the tail end, cover body and legs with slightly overlapping spearmint leaves. Cut about 10 mint leaves in half through the centre, place in position around neck. To decorate face and feet, use Tic Tacs for teeth and claws, red licorice for mouth and a mint stick thinly sliced crossways for eye and nostril.

chocolate
mint sticks

square after-
dinner mint

Stella Stegosaur

A delicious mega mint and chocolate dinosaur to set cakelovers' teeth gnashing

Snakes and Ladders

Children of all ages will be delighted with a cake that makes one of their favourite games good enough to eat

FOR THE CAKE:

3 x 340g packets buttercake mix

35cm x 45cm rectangular prepared board [page 115]

1 quantity Frosting [page 116]

450g white chocolate Melts, melted

royal blue, red and lemon yellow colourings

2/3 cup (100g) dark chocolate Melts, melted

TO DECORATE, YOU WILL NEED:

11 black licorice straps

1 large python snake

small jelly snakes

small "feet" sweets

black decorating gel

Grease 26cm x 36cm baking dish (base measurements), line base with baking paper. Using 3 packets, prepare cake mix according to the directions; pour into prepared dish. Bake in moderate oven about 1 hour. Stand cake in dish 5 minutes; turn onto wire rack to cool.

1 Using a serrated knife, level top of cake, if necessary. Place cake, baseside up, on board. Spread top and side of cake with Frosting.

2 Wrap 10 licorice straps around sides of cake.

3 Divide white chocolate Melts among 3 small bowls. Tint one portion with blue colouring, one with red, and one with yellow.

4 Quickly spread each colour onto separate sheets of baking paper in 11cm x 22cm rectangles. Just before chocolate sets, cut each rectangle into eight x 5.5cm squares.

5 Place alternate colours of chocolate squares on cake, leaving a narrow space between each horizontal row. Cut remaining licorice strap into 3 strips, place licorice strips between each row of chocolate squares.

6 Pipe dark chocolate ladder shapes on baking paper; allow to set.

7 Arrange snakes, "feet" sweets and chocolate ladders on cake. Using black decorating gel, pipe numbers on each square.

"feet" sweets

large python snake

small jelly snakes

Leonard Lion

*They'll roar for more
of this king of cakes with
the triple-treat mane*

FOR THE CAKE:

2 x 340g packets buttercake mix

3 quantities Frosting [page 116]

yellow, caramel brown and dark
brown colourings

1 tablespoon cocoa powder

35cm round prepared board
[page 115]

TO DECORATE, YOU WILL NEED:

2 white mint sweets

black decorating gel

2 green M&M's

3 strands spaghetti

1 milk chocolate Melt

1 strawberries & cream sweet

Grease deep 25cm round cake pan, line base with baking paper. Using both packets, prepare cake mix according to directions; pour into prepared pan. Bake in moderate oven about 1 hour. Stand cake in pan 5 minutes; turn onto wire rack to cool.

1 Tint Frosting with yellow colouring; divide in half. Divide one half among 3 small bowls. Tint one portion with caramel brown colouring, the second with caramel and dark brown. Tint remaining portion with dark brown, then stir in sifted cocoa.

2 Using a serrated knife, level top of cake, if necessary. Place cake, base-side up, on board. Spread top and side of cake with yellow Frosting.

3 Position a large fluted tube inside a large piping bag standing upright in a jug. Spoon all the cocoa Frosting inside bag along one side; spoon all the caramel brown Frosting next to cocoa Frosting; spoon all the dark brown Frosting down other side of bag.

4 Pipe lion's mane in swirls around edge of cake.

strawberries &
cream sweet

white mint sweets

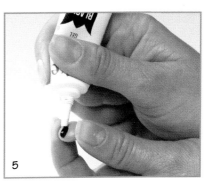

5 Make eyes by placing mints in position on cake. Using gel, pipe pupils on M&M's and secure to mints with gel.

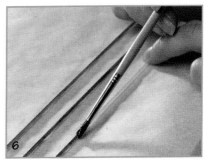

6 Make whiskers by placing spaghetti on baking paper and painting with dark brown colouring, or you can use wholemeal spaghetti. When spaghetti is dry, break into different whisker lengths.

7 Make nose by cutting milk chocolate Melt to shape and positioning on cake. Make mouth outline with gel; fill in with red part of strawberries & cream sweet. Make freckles on cheeks with gel; place spaghetti whiskers in position.

Balloon Bouquet

A carnival of colourful cakes to delight your guests. You might like to personalise each cake with the name of the birthday child

FOR THE CAKE:

2 x 340g packets buttercake mix

3 quantities Frosting [page 116]

red, pink, green, yellow, orange, blue and purple colourings

40cm square prepared board [page 115]

TO DECORATE, YOU WILL NEED:

about sixteen 50cm lengths of narrow coloured ribbons

1m of 4cm ribbon for bow

green, blue, black, red and white decorating gels

Grease 2 x 12-hole muffin pans (each hole having 1/3 cup/80ml capacity). Using 2 packets, prepare cake mix according to directions; divide mixture evenly among holes in muffin pans. Bake in moderate oven about 15 minutes. Stand in pans 5 minutes; turn onto wire racks to cool.

1 Divide Frosting among 7 small bowls. Tint Frosting red, pink, green, yellow, orange, blue and purple.

2 Insert a fork into the base of each cake to act as a handle. Spread tops and sides of cakes with Frosting. Arrange balloons on board.

3 Using a skewer, tuck ends of thin ribbon under some of the balloons. Bring other ends of all the ribbons together and tie with thick ribbon. Using decorating gel, pipe a letter on each balloon to spell out the appropriate message, if desired.

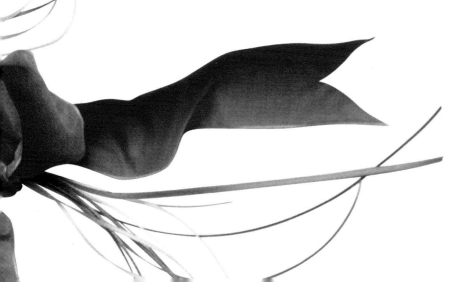

Crown of Hearts

Fit for the king or queen of the day, this cake sparkles with edible jewels

FOR THE CAKE:

3 x 340g packets buttercake mix

35cm x 45cm rectangular
    prepared board [page 115]

2 quantities Frosting [page 116]

pink colouring

TO DECORATE, YOU WILL NEED:

silver tinsel

about 35 coloured soft jubes

about 50 love hearts

10cm x 30cm piece
    silver cardboard

2 x 13g packets silver cachous

Grease 26cm x 36cm baking dish (base measurements), line base with baking paper. Using 3 packets, prepare cake mix according to directions; pour into prepared dish. Bake in moderate oven about 1 hour. Stand cake in dish 5 minutes; turn onto wire rack to cool.

love hearts

silver cachous

1 Using paper pattern, cut out crown. Using a 4.5cm cutter, cut 4 circles out of extra cake. Place cake on board.

2 Position cake circles at each point of the crown.

3 Tint Frosting with pink colouring. Spread crown with Frosting.

4 Cut tinsel into four 20cm lengths and form into circles, twisting ends together to hold the shape.

5 Using scissors, cut jubes into small pieces. Position a length of tinsel on crown; decorate with jubes.

6 Position tinsel circles; decorate cake with jubes and love hearts. Cut hearts from cardboard, position on cake; surround with silver cachous.

coloured soft jubes

CROWN OF HEARTS 13

Thomas The Tank Engine

The well-loved hero of the tiny-tot set

FOR THE CAKE:

3 x 340g packets buttercake mix

33cm x 38cm rectangular prepared board [page 115]

2 x quantities Frosting [page 116]

blue, red and black food colourings

TO DECORATE, YOU WILL NEED:

3 black licorice straps

2 x white mint sweets

black, yellow and white decorating gels

Grease 26cm x 36cm baking dish (base measurements), line base with baking paper. Using 3 packets, prepare cake mix according to directions; pour into prepared dish. Bake in moderate oven about 1 hour. Stand cake in dish 5 minutes; turn onto wire rack to cool.

1 Using paper pattern, cut out Thomas; reserve leftover cake.

2 Using a skewer or toothpick, pierce paper pattern to transfer markings onto cake. Place cake on board.

3 Cut out face; remove carefully from cake; fill hole with some of the reserved cake; put face back in position so it extends about 3cm above cake.

4 Tint half the Frosting with blue colouring. Tint a quarter of the remaining Frosting with red colouring. Tint remaining Frosting grey with black colouring. Spoon a quarter of the grey Frosting into a small bowl, tint with black colouring.

5 Following pattern, spread top and side of cake with the different Frostings, leaving Thomas' face until last.

6 Spread the circle for Thomas' face with grey Frosting.

7 Wrap a piece of licorice strap around Thomas' face. Cut licorice straps into thin strips, outline mouth, cheeks, nose, chin and engine body with strips. Paint eyeballs on mints with black decorating gel; paint eyebrows and bottom 2 bolts with black decorating gel. Outline top 2 bolts with yellow gel, position mints on face for eyes. Fill in mouth with white decorating gel.

Dreamtime Lizard

*Inspired by Aboriginal legend,
this striking cake is distinctively
an Australian original*

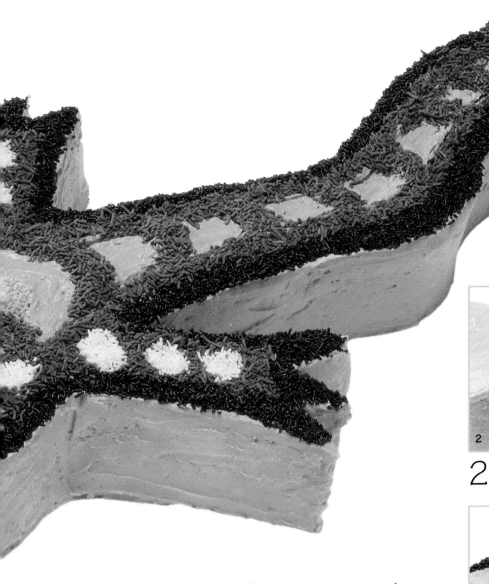

2 Tint Frosting with green colouring. Spread lizard all over with Frosting.

3 Sprinkle edge of lizard with brown sprinkles, then sketch in lizard's markings with a skewer.

Grease two 20cm x 30cm lamington pans, line the bases with baking paper. Using 3 packets, prepare cake mix according to directions; divide between prepared pans. Bake in moderate oven about 40 minutes. Stand cakes in pans 5 minutes; turn onto wire racks to cool.

FOR THE CAKE:

3 x 340g packets buttercake mix

35cm x 70cm rectangular prepared board [page 115]

2 quantities Frosting [page 116]

green colouring

TO DECORATE, YOU WILL NEED:

1 x 25g packet each brown, purple, yellow, pink, orange and blue coloured sprinkles

1 Place cakes side by side. Using paper pattern, cut out lizard. Place cakes on board, joining tail and body pieces with a little of the Frosting.

4 Sprinkle a row of purple sprinkles around the markings. Use remaining sprinkles to decorate lizard.

FOR THE CAKE:

3 x 340g packets buttercake mix

28cm round prepared board
    [page 115]

2 quantities Frosting [page 116]

red, orange and caramel colourings

TO DECORATE, YOU WILL NEED:

130g tube green Fruity Metres

small torch

1 large python snake

plastic rat

plastic spider

Grease 2 large 2.25-litre (9-cup) capacity pudding steamers. Using 3 packets, prepare cake mix according to directions; pour into prepared steamers. Bake in moderate oven about 1 hour. Stand cakes in steamers 5 minutes; turn onto wire racks to cool.

1 Using a cutter or egg-ring as a guide, cut 7cm-diameter cylindrical holes through centres of both cakes from top to base. Alternatively, remove both ends of an empty can so there is a clean, sharp edge, and use the can as a cutter to remove cylinders of cake from each cake's centre.

2 Cut one of the centre pieces in half; reserve top half for pumpkin lid.

3 Join cakes together with a little Frosting, position on board. Cut out holes for eyes, nose and mouth.

4 Tint ½ cup Frosting with red colouring. Tint remaining Frosting a deep "pumpkin" orange using orange and caramel colourings.

5 Spread cake and lid with orange Frosting. Spread inside and outer edges of mouth, eye and nose openings with red Frosting.

6 Cut some Fruity Metres into thin strips and place on cake and lid.

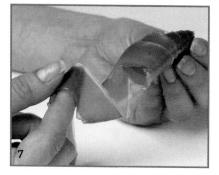

7 Roll about 50cm of Fruity Metres tightly to make stem; place on top of the lid. Just before serving, turn the torch on and secure it in centre of cake with a little Frosting. Position lid on top of cake. Decorate cake with the snake, rat and spider.

With very little trickery, you can turn two cakes baked in pudding bowls into a fabulously friendly Halloween pumpkin

Halloween Treat

Ballerinas on Stage

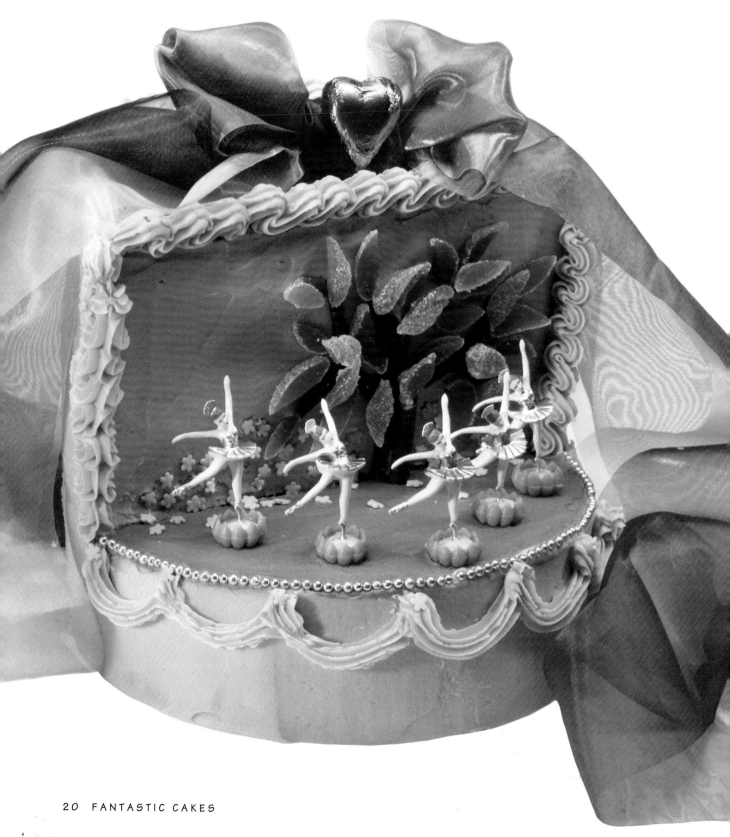

FOR THE CAKE:

3 x 340g packets buttercake mix

3 quantities Frosting [page 116]

pink, sky blue and violet colourings

35cm round prepared board
[page 115]

TO DECORATE, YOU WILL NEED:

about 15 spearmint leaves

6 chocolate mint or coffee sticks

15g packet gold cachous

coloured snowflakes

1 toothpick

1 gold-wrapped chocolate heart

1.5m each wide pink and pale pink
organza ribbon

5 plastic ballerinas

Grease 2 deep 22cm round cake pans, line the bases with baking paper. Using 3 packets, prepare cake mix according to directions; pour into prepared pans. Bake in moderate oven about 1 hour. Stand cakes in pans 5 minutes; turn onto wire racks to cool.

1 Tint half the Frosting with pink colouring in a medium bowl. Place one-third of remaining Frosting in bowl, tint with violet colouring. Tint remaining Frosting with sky blue colouring.

2 Using a serrated knife, level the tops of the cakes, if necessary. Cut one cake in half.

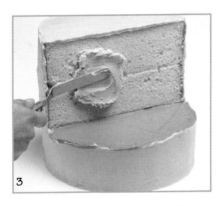

3 Position cakes on board as shown, securing together with some pink Frosting. Spread top and side of cake with coloured Frostings. Spread stage floor with violet and backdrop with some of the blue Frosting, reserving about half the blue Frosting.

4 Cut spearmint leaves in half through the centre, then cut each half into smaller leaves. Cut mint sticks in half lengthways then into various lengths for tree branches.

5 To make tree, press mint sticks and leaves gently onto backdrop.

6 Using tweezers, place cachous around front edge of stage. Spoon reserved blue Frosting into a piping bag fitted with a small fluted tube. Pipe around stage and backdrop. Sprinkle stage with snowflakes.

7 Insert toothpick into base of the chocolate heart. Tie ribbon into a bow, drape ribbon over top and sides of stage, securing bow with chocolate heart. Place ballerinas on stage.

*A ballet spectacular that will leave
any prima ballerina stagestruck*

FOR THE CAKE:

3 x 340g packets buttercake mix

35cm x 45cm rectangular
   prepared board [page 115]

2 quantities Frosting [page 116]

blue, green and red colourings

¼ cup (60ml) apricot jam,
   warmed, sieved

TO DECORATE, YOU WILL NEED:

about 50 blue M&M's

4 thin red licorice ropes

1 teaspoon yellow sprinkles

¼ cup (60g) blue sugar crystals

3 sparklers

Grease 26cm x 36cm baking dish (base measurements), line base with baking paper. Using 3 packets, prepare cake mix according to directions; pour into prepared dish. Bake in moderate oven about 1 hour. Stand cake in dish for 5 minutes; turn onto wire rack to cool.

1 Using paper pattern, cut out rocket-ship; reserve leftover cake. Place cake on prepared board.

2 Tint ¼ cup of the Frosting with blue colouring. Divide remaining Frosting in half. Tint one half with green colouring and the other with red.

3 Following pattern, spread rocket with red and green Frosting.

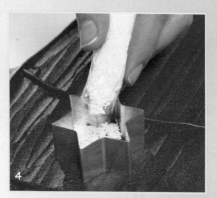

4 Use red licorice to define and decorate red area, as shown. Place a 5cm star cutter on cake, cover area inside cutter with yellow sprinkles, carefully remove cutter.

5 Mark an 8cm circle on cake, press M&M's upright around circle, then fill the circle with M&M's.

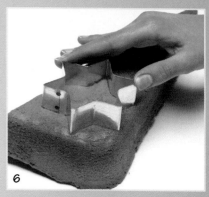

6 Cut stars from reserved cake, spread tops of stars with blue Frosting, spread sides with warm jam.

7 Sprinkle tops and sides of stars with blue crystals. Position around rocket. Position sparklers in cake; light just before serving.

Blast off! Sparks will fly when you launch this rocket

Rockin' Rocketship

Misti

We made Misti a gluten-free cake, but use a packet cake mix if you prefer

We used 100% corn rather than wheaten cornflour in this recipe. Also, it's best to use thick country-style yogurt to ensure even coverage over cake. A tub of honey yogurt can be substituted, if desired.

FOR THE CAKE:

8 eggs

1 cup (220g) caster sugar

2 cups (300g) cornflour

35cm x 45cm rectangular prepared board [page 115]

2 cups (500ml) yogurt

2 tablespoons honey

yellow colouring

1 black licorice strap

FRUIT JELLY DRESS

1 cup (250ml) orange juice

1 tablespoon caster sugar

1 tablespoon gelatine

red colouring, optional

Grease 26cm x 32cm baking dish (base measurements), line base with baking paper. Beat eggs in large bowl with electric mixer about 10 minutes, or until thick and creamy. Gradually add sugar, beating until sugar dissolves after each addition. Sift cornflour 3 times then sift cornflour over egg mixture. Gently fold cornflour into egg mixture; pour into the prepared dish. Bake in a moderate oven for about 30 minutes. Immediately turn the sponge onto a wire rack covered with baking paper to cool.

1 Make the Fruit Jelly Dress the day before cake is needed. Grease 20cm round sandwich pan, line base and sides with foil; grease foil. Combine juice and sugar in small pan, sprinkle over gelatine. Stir over low heat, without boiling, until sugar is dissolved. Boil mixture, uncovered, without stirring, 1 minute; remove from heat. Add red colouring, if desired. Strain mixture into prepared pan. Cover, refrigerate about 4 hours or overnight.

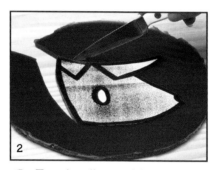

2 Turn the jelly out of the pan. Using paper pattern, trace and cut out the dress. Cut flowers from leftover jelly, if desired, to decorate board. Refrigerate until required.

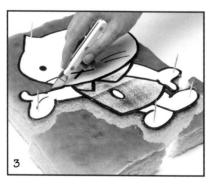

3 Using paper pattern, cut out Misti. Place cake on board.

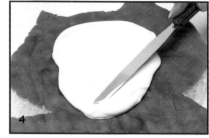

4 Combine yogurt and honey in bowl; mix well. Tint 1 tablespoon of the yogurt mixture with yellow colouring; refrigerate until required. Spread top and side of cake with white yogurt mixture. Refrigerate the cake for about 15 minutes before starting to decorate.

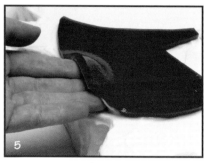

5 Place Fruit Jelly Dress in position on the cake.

6 Cut licorice into thin strips and 2 small circles for eyes.

7 About an hour before serving, outline Misti with licorice strips as shown. Pipe yellow yogurt on Fruit Jelly Dress for button. Position licorice circles for eyes. Cut 2 small pieces of licorice for mouth and whiskers.

Sunflower Power

Watch their eyes light up for this happy, smiling flower

FOR THE CAKE:

2 x 340g packets buttercake mix

500g packet ready-made icing

icing sugar mixture

lemon yellow, golden yellow and red colourings

1 quantity Frosting [page 116]

35cm round prepared board [page 115]

TO DECORATE, YOU WILL NEED:

45g Wagon Wheel

¼ teaspoon yellow sugar crystals

1.5m x 4cm green ribbon

1 chocolate bee

10cm thin wire

Grease deep 25cm round cake pan, line base with baking paper. Using both packets, prepare cake mix according to directions; pour into prepared pan. Bake in moderate oven about 1 hour. Stand cake in pan 5 minutes; turn onto wire rack to cool.

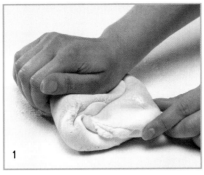

1 On a surface dusted with icing sugar, knead icing until smooth and pliable. Tint icing with lemon and golden yellow colourings; knead until both colourings are evenly distributed through icing.

2 Roll icing out evenly to about 2mm thick. Using petal patterns below, cut out about 25 small, 25 medium and 25 large petal shapes.

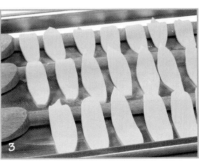

3 Drape ends of petals over wooden spoon handles and allow to dry.

4 Tint Frosting with golden yellow and a little red colouring. Using a serrated knife, level top of cake. Place cake, base-side up, on board. Spread cake with Frosting.

5 Leave enough space for Wagon Wheel in centre of the cake. Press petals gently into Frosting, using large petals for outer row, then a row of medium petals, then a row of small petals.

6 Place Wagon Wheel in centre of cake; sprinkle with yellow sugar crystals. Secure ribbon around cake. Insert wire into bee and position on cake.

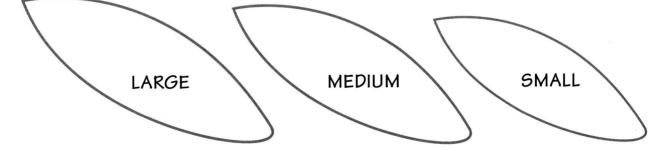

LARGE   MEDIUM   SMALL

FOR THE CAKE:

2 x 340g packets buttercake mix

35cm round prepared board
  [page 115]

1 quantity Frosting [page 116]

violet and orange colourings

TO DECORATE, YOU WILL NEED:

1 black licorice strap

11 green Smarties

2 white mint sweets

2 blue Smarties

about 150g sour jelly worms

Grease deep 25cm round cake pan, line base with baking paper. Using both packets, prepare cake mix according to directions; pour into prepared pan. Bake in moderate oven about 1 hour. Stand cake in pan 5 minutes; turn onto wire rack to cool.

1 Using paper pattern, cut out face. Place cake on board.

2 Tint three-quarters of the Frosting with orange colouring; then tint remainder with violet colouring. Following pattern, spread cake with orange and violet Frosting.

3 Cut licorice strap into thin strips; position licorice strips for mouth as shown. Cut a small piece off each green Smartie and position the larger pieces for teeth.

4 Place mints in position for eyes. Secure blue Smarties onto mints with Frosting.

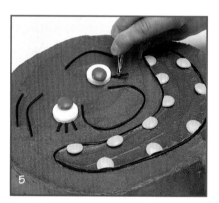

5 Position remaining licorice as shown. Insert jelly worms into top of head for hair.

sour jelly worms

Kids love funny faces so Merv is bound to create peals of merriment

Merv the Nerd

The Big Top

1 Using a serrated knife, level top of smaller cake, mark a circle on top about 2cm from edge. Cut out circle and remove centre; reserve centre piece. Place cake ring on board.

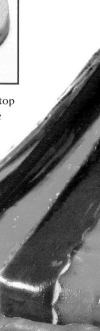

FOR THE CAKE:

3 x 340g packets buttercake mix

30cm round prepared board [page 115]

1 quantity Frosting [page 116]

TO DECORATE, YOU WILL NEED:

mixed lollies

strawberry, tropical and apple Fruity Metres

red shoestring licorice

four 6cm candy canes

1 toothpick

1 cup (90g) toasted desiccated coconut

clown candles

Grease deep 20cm round and deep 22cm round cake pans. Using the 3 packets, prepare cake mix according to directions; fill 20cm pan to 2cm below rim of pan. Pour remaining mixture into 22cm pan. Bake both cakes in moderate oven about 1 hour. Stand cakes in pans 5 minutes; turn onto wire racks to cool.

2 Place reserved centre piece on top of larger cake. Shape the whole cake into a cone resembling the roof of a tent top. Secure with a little Frosting.

3 Fill centre of smaller cake with lollies. Spread Frosting over tent roof; reserve about 1 tablespoon of the Frosting.

4 Measure height of side of tent, cut 24 pieces of each colour of Fruity Metres to that length; position around the side of the tent. Measure roof, cut 24 pieces of each colour of Fruity Metres to fit; position on roof.

5 Cut a 70cm strip of yellow Fruity Metres and cut 1 edge into scallops. Brush with a little water and attach to edge of roof. Place roof in position. Fold 2 rolls of tropical Fruity Metres in half lengthways, twist to form a coil; brush with water. Wrap around edge of roof and base of tent. Secure two ends at front to form curtains. Position red licorice ropes and candy cane tent pegs with a little of the reserved Frosting. Attach a flag made from pieces of Fruity Metres on a toothpick; sprinkle ground with coconut and position clowns.

Geraldine Giraffe

This cake would be the perfect choice for a zoo theme party

FOR THE CAKE:

3 x 340g packets buttercake mix

35cm x 50cm rectangular prepared board [page 115]

1½ quantities Frosting [page 116]

red and buttercup yellow colouring

TO DECORATE, YOU WILL NEED:

2 black licorice straps

Fruit Tango Fruity Metres:
3 x 27cm strips, 1 x 20cm strip

toothpick

6cm piece licorice twists

1 black jelly bean

1 chocolate bullet

2/3 cup (100g) milk chocolate Melts, melted

Grease 26cm x 36cm baking dish (base measurements), line base with baking paper. Using 3 packets, prepare cake mix according to directions; pour into prepared dish. Bake in moderate oven about 1 hour. Stand cake in dish for 5 minutes; turn onto wire rack to cool.

1 Using paper pattern, cut out the body and head of the giraffe. Place cake on prepared board.

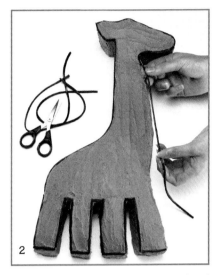

2 Tint Frosting brown with red and buttercup yellow colourings. Join head and body of giraffe with a little Frosting, spread cake with remaining Frosting. Cut 1 licorice strap into thin strips; position licorice around cake.

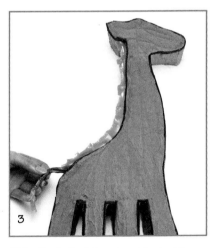

3 Stick the 3 lengths of Fruity Metres together to make 1 thick length; cut into long thin strips but not all the way through to the base; position on giraffe for mane. Cut a 1cm x 8cm piece of licorice strap. Wrap 20cm Fruity Metre around licorice to cover tail; cut end of Fruity Metre to fray end. Secure tail with a toothpick.

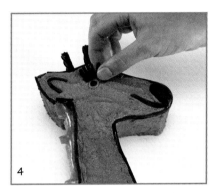

4 Cut some of the remaining licorice strap into thin strips, position on cake for ear and mouth. Cut licorice twists in half, position for horns. Cut jelly bean in half lengthways, position for nose. Cut chocolate bullet in half, position for eye. Cut a 1cm x 2cm piece of licorice strap into thin strips – do not cut through base – position for eyelash.

5 Cover oven tray with baking paper, spread melted chocolate evenly to make a 20cm square. When chocolate is almost set, cut into 2.5cm diamond shapes. When chocolate is completely set, gently lift diamonds off paper; position on giraffe as shown.

Starstruck

FOR THE CAKE:

3 x 340g packets buttercake mix

1¼ cups (185g) white chocolate Melts, melted

2 teaspoons vegetable oil

yellow, green, blue and pink sugar crystals

45cm round prepared board [page 115]

1 cup (150g) white chocolate Melts, melted, extra

1½ quantities Frosting [page 116]

purple and pink colourings

TO DECORATE, YOU WILL NEED:

yellow, green, blue and pink sugar crystals

white chocolate Melts

Grease deep 20cm round and deep 22cm round cake pans, line bases with baking paper. Using 3 packets, prepare cake mix according to directions; pour into prepared pans. Bake both cakes in moderate oven about 1 hour. Stand cakes in pans 5 minutes; turn onto wire racks to cool.

1 Combine melted chocolate and oil in small bowl. Spread chocolate onto baking paper until about 2mm thick, leave until almost set. Using a 5cm round cutter and a 7cm star cutter, cut chocolate into 3 rounds and 17 stars. It may be necessary to remelt and respread leftover chocolate to obtain all 17 stars.

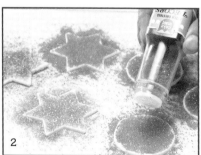

2 Place stars and rounds on oven trays covered with baking paper. Sprinkle shapes generously with sugar crystals. To make sure the crystals stick to the chocolate, heat the shapes in moderate oven for 2 minutes or until chocolate melts slightly but still retains its shape. Remove from oven, leave to set.

3 Trace 2 Saturn rings on baking paper, outline by piping with extra chocolate, fill rings with chocolate. If chocolate begins to set too quickly, place rings in moderate oven about 2 minutes or until chocolate melts slightly, but still retains its shape. Remove from oven, leave to set.

Take the kids on a space odyssey to the beautiful planet Saturn

4 Tint half the Frosting with pink colouring, tint the remainder with purple colouring. Reserve about ¼ cup purple Frosting. Place large cake on board. Spoon the pink and purple Frosting onto cake, gently swirl over cake for a marbled effect. Sprinkle with pink sugar crystals.

5 Using a serrated knife, level top of small cake to make it 4cm thick; discard leftover top of cake. Using a 3cm round cutter, cut 16 rounds from remaining cake. Level tops of rounds so they are about 4cm high.

6 Cut 4 of the cake rounds in half. Use reserved Frosting to secure cake rounds to board around cake, and to secure chocolate stars and circles on cake rounds. Position chocolate Saturn rings on cake.

Blooming Beauty

FOR THE CAKE:

3 x 340g packets buttercake mix

2 quantities Frosting [page 116]

red, yellow and caramel brown
   colourings

35cm round prepared board
   [page 115]

TO DECORATE, YOU WILL NEED:

chocolate thins

silk flowers

silk butterflies

1 metre ribbon for bow

Grease 2 deep 22cm round cake pans
and 1 deep 20cm round cake pan, line
bases with baking paper. Using the
3 packets, prepare cake mix according to
directions; divide mixture evenly among
prepared pans. Bake cakes in moderate
oven about 35 minutes for the 20cm cake
and about 45 minutes for the 22cm cakes.
Stand cakes in pan 5 minutes; turn onto
wire racks to cool.

1 Tint Frosting brown, using red, yellow and caramel brown colourings.

2 Place the small cake on top of one
of the large cakes. Using a sharp
knife and the small cake as a guide, cut
large cake into a ring.

3 Cut ring in half horizontally; reserve one half, discard the other.

4 Place the small cake on remaining
large cake, cut a circle 2cm deep,
using the small cake as a guide.

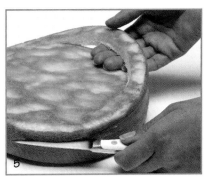

5 Remove small cake. Cut through
the side of the large cake to about
a third of the way down, remove and
discard the ring-shaped piece of cake.

6 Place the reserved ring of cake on
board. Place the 2 small cakes
inside the ring, top with the large piece
of cake to form a rim.

7 Trim the edge of the large cake on
a slight angle.

8 Spread cake with Frosting.
Sprinkle chocolate thins in centre
of cake for the soil. Position flowers and
butterflies, and tie ribbon in a bow.

*Nifty cake cutting makes
the pot, and silk flowers top
this pretty posy*

Graffiti Unlimited

FOR THE CAKE:

2 x 340g packets buttercake mix

25cm x 35cm rectangular
   prepared board [page 115]

1 quantity Chocolate Frosting
   [page 116]

brown, black and green colourings

TO DECORATE, YOU WILL NEED:

1 matchbox

1 tablespoon icing sugar mixture

1 tablespoon drinking chocolate

2 x 30g bars chocolate Flake

¼ cup (35g) milk chocolate Melts,
   melted

2 chocolate mint sticks

¼ cup (35g) white chocolate
   Melts, melted

yellow decorating icing

white decorating gel

⅓ cup (35g) desiccated coconut

5 boiled sweets

Grease deep 23cm square cake pan, line base with baking paper. Using 2 packets, prepare cake mix according to directions; pour into prepared pan. Bake in moderate oven about 1 hour. Stand cake in pan 5 minutes; turn onto wire rack to cool.

1 Using a serrated knife, cut a 3cm slice from one side of cake. Tint Frosting with brown colouring.

2 Spread cut side of large cake with Frosting; place cake, Frosting side down, on board. Spread Frosting along one end of remaining cake slice; place cake directly in front of large cake.

3 Cut chunks out of top of cake at random. Spread cake and board with Frosting.

4 Wrap matchbox cover with foil, leaving ends open. Dip one end of matchbox in combined icing sugar and drinking chocolate, press gently into Frosting to form brickwork pattern.

5 To make telegraph pole, place one Flake on a piece of baking paper, cut remaining Flake in half. Secure half of Flake on one end of whole Flake with a little milk chocolate. Secure mint sticks to Flake with a little more chocolate. Leave to dry before attaching to board with a little more chocolate.

flake

chocolate mint stick

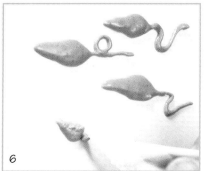

6 To make the mice, tint the white chocolate grey with black colouring. Pipe mice shapes onto a piece of baking paper; leave to set.

boiled sweets

7 Using yellow decorating icing, pipe a "paint splash" on wall. Pipe graffiti on remaining wall with white decorating gel. Tint coconut with green colouring, sprinkle coconut around base of cake. Spread crushed boiled sweets over board to resemble broken glass. Arrange mice and toys of your choice around wall.

Personalise the messages scrawled all over this clever cake, which looks just like an inner-city wall

A puff of fairy floss makes a soft and cuddly chest for this lovable southern visitor

FOR THE CAKE:

3 x 340g packets buttercake mix

35cm x 45cm rectangular prepared board [page 115]

2 quantities Frosting [page 116]

true blue, yellow and orange colourings

TO DECORATE, YOU WILL NEED:

2 slices crystallised orange

1 mint

1 red jelly bean

1 black licorice strap

1/2 x 30g packet pink fairy floss

50cm x 4cm pink wired ribbon

Grease 26cm x 36cm baking dish (base measurements), line base and sides with baking paper. Using 3 packets, prepare cake mix according to directions; pour into prepared dish. Bake in moderate oven about 1 hour. Stand cake in dish 5 minutes; turn onto wire rack to cool.

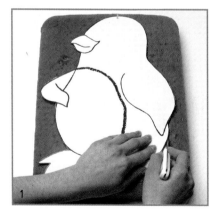

1 Using paper pattern, cut out the penguin. Place cake on board.

2 Tint half the Frosting with true blue colouring. Divide the remaining half among 3 small bowls; tint one with yellow colouring, one with orange colouring and leave the third plain.

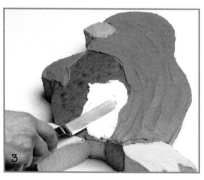

3 Spread top and sides of cake with coloured Frosting as shown.

4 Remove the rind from crystallised orange slices; using paper pattern, cut pieces to shape of beak. Press gently into position.

5 To make eye, place the mint in position, then secure half the red jelly bean to mint with Frosting.

6 To make eyelash, cut licorice strap into a 1.5cm x 3cm rectangle, then cut into thin strips – do not cut all the way through the strap.

7 Fan licorice piece, place in position in a slight curve above the eye.

8 Using scissors, cut the remaining licorice strap into several thin strips. Position strips to outline the stomach, wings, beak and feet. Just before serving, press fairy floss on stomach. (Fairy floss starts to dissolve after about an hour.) Tie ribbon into a bow, position on cake.

Peggy Penguin

FOR THE COTTAGE:

375g butter, chopped

1½ cups (300g) firmly packed
   dark brown sugar

⅓ cup (75g) caster sugar

1 egg

1 egg white

¾ cup (180ml) molasses

1 cup (250ml) chocolate topping

1.2kg (8 cups) plain flour

¾ cup (75g) cocoa powder

1 tablespoon ground cinnamon

2 teaspoons ground ginger

1 teaspoon ground cloves

1½ teaspoons bicarbonate of soda

assorted sweets and licorice

ROYAL ICING

6 egg whites

1.5kg (9½ cups) pure icing sugar,
   approximately

1 teaspoon lemon juice

50cm x 60cm rectangular
   prepared board [page 115]

Beat butter and sugars in large bowl with electric mixer until combined and just beginning to change colour. Add egg, egg white, molasses and topping; beat until smooth. Stir in the sifted dry ingredients with wooden spoon to form a smooth dough. Divide mixture into 6 portions, roll each portion into a ball; flatten slightly. Wrap each portion in plastic wrap; refrigerate 1 hour.

1 On a lightly floured sheet of baking paper, roll out each portion of dough to 5mm thick. Using paper patterns and a small sharp knife, cut out walls and roof. Place gingerbread pieces on oven trays covered with baking paper. Bake in moderately slow oven about 40 minutes or until firm; cool on trays.

2 Royal Icing: Beat egg whites in a large bowl on low speed with an electric mixer until foamy. Gradually beat in sifted icing sugar, about a heaped tablespoonful at a time, until icing is thick and spreadable; stir in lemon juice. Cover icing with plastic wrap, pressing plastic down firmly onto the surface of the icing to prevent it from drying out during use.

3 Working with one gingerbread piece at a time, spread with a generous layer of Royal Icing. Position sweets and licorice firmly in Icing. Stand about an hour for Icing to set.

A gingerbread house that's almost too pretty to eat, but try telling the kids that!

Candy Cottage

4 Assemble house on board, using Icing to hold walls together. Place tumblers inside house, at each corner, to help support walls while Icing sets.

5 Attach roof panels to walls with Icing. Use tall tumblers under the eaves to support the roof until set. Place a row of sweets or licorice strip along ridge of roof.

6 Spread remaining icing on board, decorate with more sweets and licorice for grass, fence and pathway.

Humphrey

This funny old fella is a classic hit among children

FOR THE CAKE:

3 x 340g packets buttercake mix

35cm x 45cm rectangular prepared board [page 115]

1 quantity Frosting [page 116]

red, yellow and brown colourings

1 quantity chocolate Frosting [page 116]

1 cup (90g) desiccated coconut

TO DECORATE, YOU WILL NEED:

1/3 cup (50g) dark chocolate Melts

3 x chocolate Monte biscuits

2 black licorice straps

Grease 26cm x 36cm baking dish (base measurements), line base with baking paper. Using 3 packets, prepare cake mix according to directions; pour into prepared dish. Bake in moderate oven about 1 hour. Stand cake in dish 5 minutes; turn onto wire rack to cool.

1 Using paper pattern, cut Humphrey out of cooled cake.

2 Place cake on board. Using a toothpick or skewer, mark in outlines of bow tie and hat.

3 Reserve 1/3 cup of the Frosting; tint remaining Frosting with yellow colouring. Tint half of the reserved Frosting with red colouring, leave remaining half white. Tint chocolate Frosting with brown colouring.

4 Stir the coconut into chocolate Frosting. Spread Humphrey's face with chocolate Frosting.

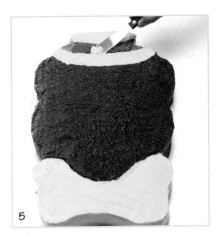

5 Use yellow and red Frosting for Humphrey's hat and bow tie.

6 Reserving 2 chocolate Melts, melt the remainder. Cut biscuits to make the shape of the nose. Place on tray covered with baking paper. Join biscuits with melted chocolate. Spread remaining melted chocolate all over biscuits. Allow to set; position on face.

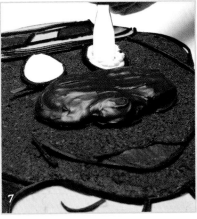

7 Cut licorice straps into thin strips. Position licorice to form outline of eyes and mouth. Use red Frosting for mouth and white Frosting for eyes and top of nose. Position remaining licorice strips as shown. Position reserved chocolate Melts for pupils.

Heart of Hearts

FOR THE CAKE:

3 x 340g packets buttercake mix

2 quantities Frosting [page 116]

rose petal pink colouring

40cm round prepared board
[page 115]

TO DECORATE, YOU WILL NEED:

4m each of yellow, orange, pink
and purple satin cord

20 x 35cm long thin wire

2/3 cup (100g) white chocolate
Melts, melted

10 small love heart sweets,
in assorted colours

10 large love heart sweets,
in assorted colours

7cm round cutter or an egg ring

4m orange organza ribbon

2m x 5cm pink wire ribbon

2m gold-edged orange
organza ribbon

2m each of hot pink and purple
organza ribbon

Grease 7cm deep x 30.5cm heart cake
pan, line base with baking paper.
Using 3 packets, prepare cake
mix according to directions;
pour into prepared pan.
Bake in moderate oven
about 1¼ hours. Stand
cake in pan 5 minutes;
turn onto wire rack
to cool.

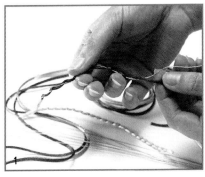

1 Twist yellow cord around 5 pieces of wire, cutting and securing cord at end of each piece of wire. Continue wrapping wire with remaining 3 colours of cord; you will have 5 pieces of cord-wrapped wire in each of the 4 cord colours. Reserve remaining cord.

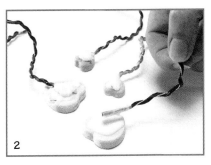

2 Spread a little melted chocolate on the back of each heart, place wire in centre of chocolate, stand until set.

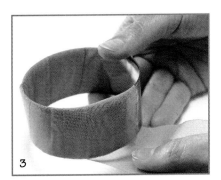

3 Cover cutter or egg ring with half the orange organza ribbon.

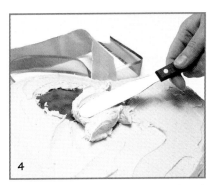

4 Tint Frosting with rose petal pink colouring. Place cake on board, spread with Frosting.

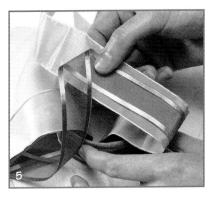

5 Position cutter in centre of cake. Wrap pink wire ribbon and gold-edged orange organza ribbon over side and top of cake, bringing them up through the cutter. Arrange remaining orange organza ribbon with the hot pink and purple organza ribbon in centre of cutter. Twist remaining cord into a single plait, wrap around base of cake.

*A message of love
in a heart-shaped
cake bedecked with
ribbons and sweets*

large love heart sweets

small love heart sweets

FOR THE CAKE:

3 x 340g packets buttercake mix

2 quantities Frosting [page 116]

green and orange colourings

40cm round prepared board
   [page 115]

TO DECORATE, YOU WILL NEED:

2 x white mint sweets

2 x blue M&M's

red decorating gel

1 black licorice strap

1 crystallised orange slice

Grease deep 30cm round cake pan, line base with baking paper. Using 3 packets, prepare cake mix according to directions; pour into prepared pan. Bake in moderate oven about 1¼ hours. Stand cake in pan 5 minutes; turn onto wire rack to cool.

1 Leave a quarter of the Frosting white. Divide remaining Frosting between 2 bowls; tint one portion with green colouring and the other with orange.

2 Using paper pattern, cut out cat; discard scraps. Place cake on board.

3 Following pattern, spread hat with green Frosting. Spread face and ears with orange Frosting. Spread mouth area with white Frosting.

4 For eyes, place mints in position, secure M&M's in centre of mints with Frosting for pupils.

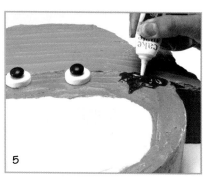

5 Using the red decorating gel, pipe on clumps of hair.

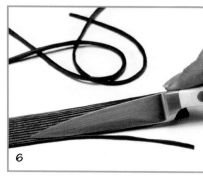

6 Cut licorice into thin strips for whiskers and mouth. Cut crystallised orange for the nose.

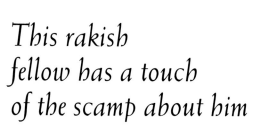

This rakish fellow has a touch of the scamp about him

Hairy Scary Spider

FOR THE CAKE:

2 x 340g packets buttercake mix

40cm square prepared board
    [page 115]

2 quantities Chocolate Frosting
    [page 116]

brown colouring

1 cup (70g) shredded coconut

TO DECORATE, YOU WILL NEED:

1⅓ cups (200g) milk chocolate
    Melts, melted

2 red Smarties

2 milk chocolate Melts, extra

5 milk Choc Bits

red decorating gel

black decorating gel, optional

Grease 2 deep 20cm round cake pans, line bases with baking paper. Using both packets, prepare cake mix according to directions; divide between prepared pans. Bake in moderate oven about 50 minutes. Stand cakes in pans 5 minutes; turn onto wire racks to cool.

1 Cut a 12cm round out of a piece of baking paper; use to cut out spider's head from one of the cakes.

2 Tint chocolate Frosting with the brown colouring; stir in coconut.

3 Position cakes on board. Spread the spider's head and body with Frosting, building up 4 mounds for eyes and pincers, as shown.

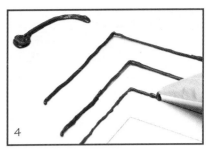

4 Draw 8 legs and 2 pincers on a piece of baking paper. Pipe over markings with melted chocolate. Once chocolate has set, pipe another layer of chocolate over the legs to make them thicker. Repeat once more; leave to set.

5 To make main eyes, attach Smarties to the 2 extra Melts with Frosting and position as shown on mounds. Make a row of 5 smaller eyes with Choc Bits and mark centres with red decorating gel.

6 Position the legs and pincers in Frosting. Draw in web with black decorating gel, if desired.

Let them sink their teeth into this monster — there's nothing to be scared of really

A Different Drummer

An easy shape, this cake is sure to hit the right note

FOR THE CAKE:

3 x 340g packets buttercake mix

2 quantities Frosting [page 116]

royal blue and red colouring

35cm round prepared board
    [page 115]

500g packet ready-made icing

icing sugar mixture

TO DECORATE, YOU WILL NEED:

200g red licorice Super Ropes

8 white Kool Mints

2 x 12cm red-and-white striped
    candy canes (or sticks)

Grease 2 deep 20cm round cake pans, line bases with baking paper. Using the 3 packets, prepare cake mix according to directions; divide mixture evenly between prepared pans. Bake in moderate oven about 1 hour. Stand cakes in pans 5 minutes; turn onto wire racks to cool. Using a serrated knife, level tops of cakes.

1 Tint two-thirds of the Frosting with royal blue colouring. Sandwich tops of cakes together with a little of the blue Frosting. Place cake on board.

2 Spread top of cake with the white Frosting; spread around side with blue Frosting.

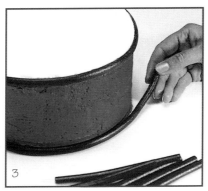

3 Wrap rope around base and top edge of drum (you may need to secure rope with toothpicks).

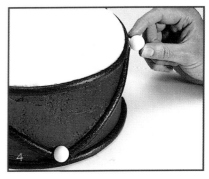

4 Cut remaining rope into eight 14cm lengths; place around side of drum as shown. Place the Kool Mints in position.

5 On a surface dusted with icing sugar, knead ready-made icing until smooth and pliable. Tint with red colouring. Roll icing into 2 balls for drumsticks, wrap tightly in plastic wrap and stand about 1 hour or until firm. If using candy canes, snap off crook of neck, leaving 12cm length of stick; insert broken ends into balls. Position drumsticks on top of cake.

red-and-white striped
candy cane

No wonder this colourful little cartoon character has such a loyal following — the eyes have it!

FOR THE CAKE:

3 x 340g packets buttercake mix

40cm square prepared board [page 115]

2 quantities Frosting [page 116]

black, royal blue, orange, yellow and buttercup yellow food colourings

TO DECORATE, YOU WILL NEED:

chocolate decorating gel

1 black licorice strap

Grease deep 30cm square cake pan, line base with baking paper. Using 3 packets, prepare cake mix according to directions; pour into prepared pan. Bake in moderate oven about 1¼ hours. Stand cake in pan 5 minutes; turn onto wire rack to cool.

1 Using paper pattern, cut out Tweety. Place cake on board.

2 Using a metal skewer of toothpick, pierce paper pattern to transfer an outline of markings onto cake.

3 Tint 2 tablespoons of the Frosting with black colouring, ¼ cup Frosting with royal blue, ⅓ cup Frosting with orange and leave ⅓ cup Frosting white. Tint remaining Frosting with both yellow and orange colourings.

4 Following pattern outlines for the face, beak and eyes, spread Frosting on the cake.

5 Using chocolate decorating gel, outline beak and eyes; draw in the eyebrows and eyelashes. Cut licorice strap into thin strips to create Tweety's stylised feather topknot.

TM & © 1998 Warner Bros

Tweety Bird

FOR THE CAKE:

4 x 340g packets buttercake mix

45cm square prepared board
    [page 115]

2 quantities Frosting [page 116]

black, red, terracotta and brown
    colourings

TO DECORATE, YOU WILL NEED:

1 black licorice strap

black and white decorating gels

Grease 2 deep 23cm square cake pans,
line bases with baking paper. Using the
4 packets, prepare cake mix according to
directions; divide mixture between
prepared pans. Bake in moderate oven
about 1 hour. Stand cakes in pans for
5 minutes; turn onto wire racks to cool.

2 Using paper pattern, cut Sylvester
out of arranged cakes.

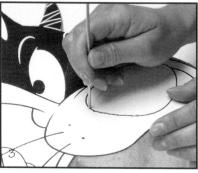

3 Using a toothpick or skewer, pierce
paper pattern to transfer outlines of
markings onto the cake.

1 Cut 1 cake in half. Position cakes on
board as shown, securing the pieces
together with a little Frosting.

Sylvester

the Cat

4 Tint ⅓ cup Frosting with black colouring, ⅓ cup Frosting with red colouring, ¼ cup Frosting a dark terracotta colour with terracotta and brown colourings, ¼ cup a lighter terracotta colour with lesser amounts of the terracotta and brown colourings, and leave remaining Frosting white.

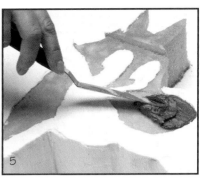

5 Spread Sylvester's face, inside left ear and eyes with white Frosting as shown; nose with red; tongue with light terracotta; mouth with dark terracotta; and remaining area with black.

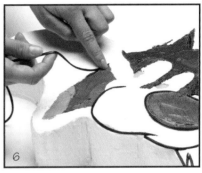

6 Cut licorice strap into thin strips. Outline Sylvester's features with licorice. Use black decorating gel for pupils of eyes and white decorating gel for the eyebrows.

*"Suffering succotash,
now I'm a cake!"*

FOR THE CAKE:

4 x 340g packets buttercake mix

45cm square prepared board
   [page 115]

2 quantities Frosting [page 116]

buttercup yellow, black, terracotta
   and brown colourings

TO DECORATE, YOU WILL NEED:

1 black licorice strap

black and white decorating gels

Grease 2 deep 23cm square cake pans, line bases with baking paper. Using the 4 packets, prepare cake mix according to directions; divide mixture between prepared pans. Bake in moderate oven about 1 hour. Stand cakes in pans for 5 minutes; turn onto wire racks to cool.

1 Cut 1 cake in half. Position cakes on board as shown, securing together with a little Frosting.

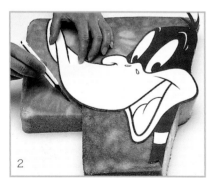

2 Using paper pattern, cut Daffy out of arranged cakes.

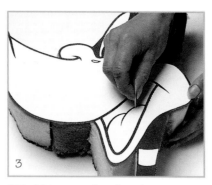

3 Using a toothpick or skewer, pierce paper pattern to transfer outlines of markings onto the cake.

4 Tint half the Frosting with buttercup yellow colouring, then tint half of the remaining Frosting with black colouring. Divide the remainder into 3 portions: tint 1 portion a dark terracotta with terracotta and brown colourings, another portion a lighter terracotta colour with lesser amounts of the terracotta and brown colourings and leave remaining Frosting white.

5 Spread Daffy's tongue with light terracotta; his mouth with dark terracotta; and beak with yellow Frosting. Use black Frosting for remaining body, and white for eyes and band around neck.

6 Cut licorice strap into thin strips. Outline Daffy's features with licorice. Use black decorating gel for pupils of eyes and white decorating gel for eyebrows.

Daffy Duck

There'th nothing dithpicable
about thith delithshus cake

FOR THE CAKE:

3 x 340g packets buttercake mix

35cm x 45cm rectangular
   prepared board [page 115]

1 quantity Frosting [page 116]

royal blue colouring

TO DECORATE, YOU WILL NEED:

blue and white sugar crystals

1 black licorice strap

1 blue M&M

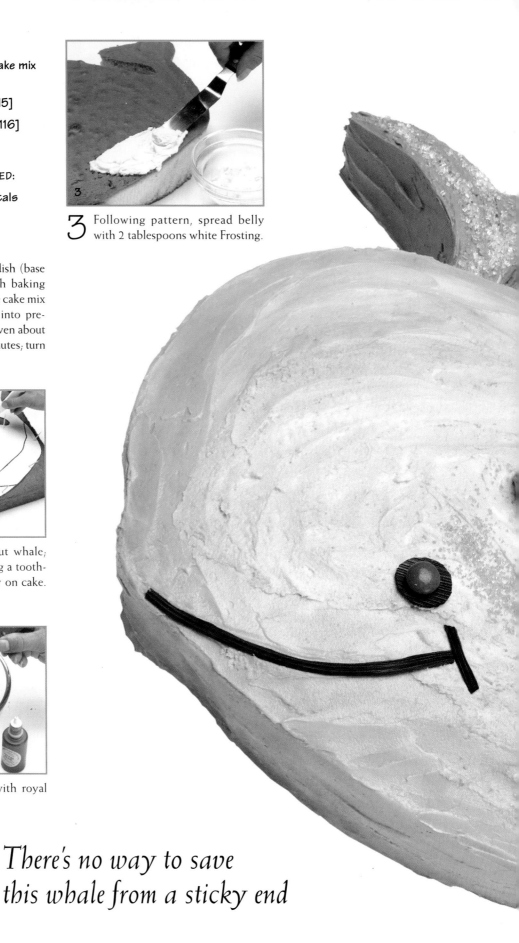

3 Following pattern, spread belly
   with 2 tablespoons white Frosting.

Grease 26cm x 36cm baking dish (base measurements), line base with baking paper. Using 3 packets, prepare cake mix according to directions; pour into pre-pared dish. Bake in moderate oven about 1 hour. Stand cake in dish 5 minutes; turn onto wire rack to cool.

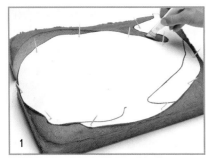

1 Use paper pattern, cut out whale;
   reserve leftover cake. Using a tooth-pick or skewer, mark out belly on cake. Place cake on board.

2 Tint half the Frosting with royal
   blue colouring.

*There's no way to save
this whale from a sticky end*

Wally Whale

4 Swirl blue Frosting into remaining white Frosting gently to create a marbled effect. Carefully spread marbled Frosting on cake.

5 Cut spout and flipper from reserved leftover cake and position on cake; spread with more Frosting.

6 Sprinkle blue sugar crystals on and around the flipper, tail and belly. Sprinkle white sugar crystals on spout. Cut a thin strip of licorice for mouth and place in position. Cut eye from remaining licorice; position on cake. Secure blue M&M on licorice with Frosting.

Spot

This lovable little puppy
turns up everywhere

Grease 26cm x 36cm baking dish (base measurements), line base with baking paper. Using 3 packets, prepare cake mix according to directions; pour into prepared dish. Bake in moderate oven about 1 hour. Stand cake in dish 5 minutes; turn onto wire rack to cool.

1 Using paper pattern, cut out Spot. Place cake on board.

2 Tint a quarter of the Frosting with royal blue colouring for the gift box; tint remainder with both caramel and buttercup yellow colourings to match Spot's coat.

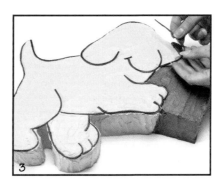

3 Following pattern, spread top and side of cake with Frosting. Cut some of the licorice strap into thin strips. Position strips to outline body, paws and Spot's facial features.

4 To make spot and tail, trace tail outline on baking paper, spread melted chocolate on baking paper to fill outline. Spread remaining chocolate on baking paper in a 5cm circle. Just before it sets, use a 4cm round cutter to cut chocolate into a neat circle. Position spot and tail on cake.

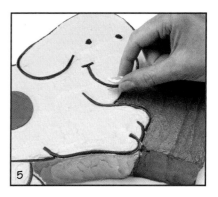

5 Position currants for eyes; quarter the jelly bean and use ¼ jelly bean for the tongue.

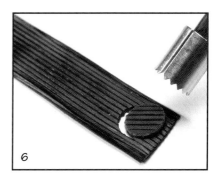

6 To make nose, use an apple corer to cut licorice into a circle. Place on cake. Decorate gift box with the ribbon and red M&M's.

Copyright © Eric Hill/Salspot 1998
This cake may not be reproduced, manufactured or made up for resale or for any other commercial purpose without the express written consent of Ventura Publishing Ltd.

FOR THE CAKE:

3 x 340g packets buttercake mix

35cm x 45cm rectangular prepared board [page 115]

1 quantity Frosting [page 116]

caramel, buttercup yellow and royal blue colourings

TO DECORATE, YOU WILL NEED:

1 black licorice strap

25g milk chocolate Melts, melted

2 dried currants

1 pink jelly bean

40cm x 1cm white ribbon

10 red M&M's

Supercool Superstar

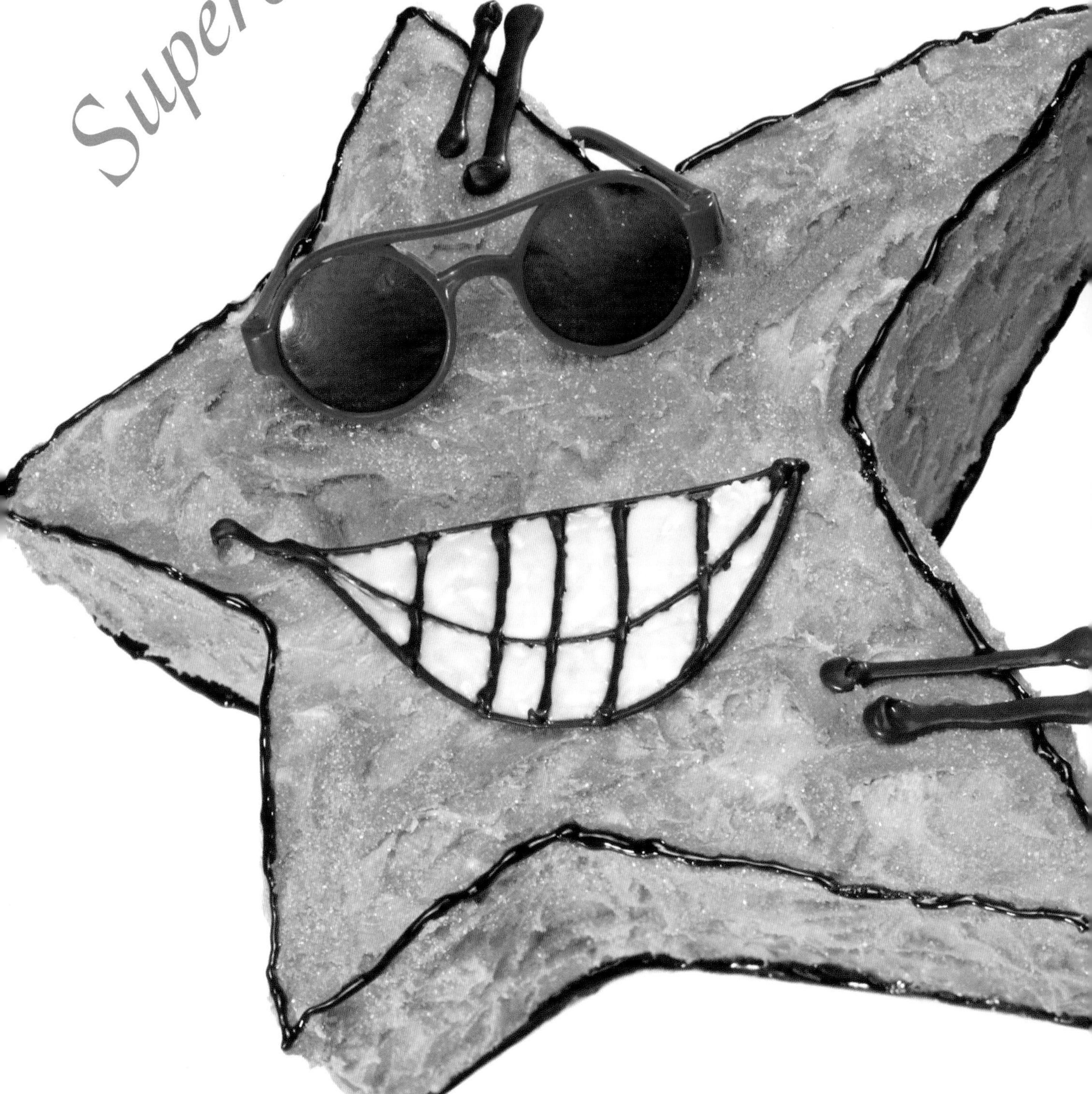

FOR THE CAKE:

4 x 340g packets buttercake mix

40cm square prepared board [page 115]

2 quantities Frosting [page 116]

buttercup yellow, orange and lemon yellow colourings

TO DECORATE, YOU WILL NEED:

yellow sugar crystals

1/3 cup (50g) dark chocolate Melts, melted

1/2 cup (75g) white chocolate Melts, melted

brown decorating gel

child's sunglasses

Grease deep 30cm square cake pan, line base with baking paper. Using 4 packets, prepare cake mix according to directions; pour into prepared pan. Bake in moderate oven about 1 3/4 hours. Stand cake in pan 5 minutes; turn onto wire rack to cool.

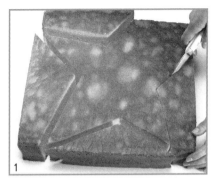

1 Place cake on board. Using paper pattern, cut out a star shape, or cut a freeform star to your liking.

2 Divide Frosting into 3 portions; tint 1 portion with buttercup yellow, 1 portion with orange colouring, and 1 portion with lemon yellow colouring.

3 Combine the three Frostings in a medium bowl and swirl gently to create a marbled effect.

4 Spread top and sides of star with marbled Frosting. Sprinkle star with sugar crystals.

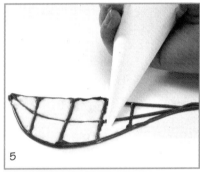

5 Pipe melted dark chocolate outline for mouth onto baking paper; pipe pairs of straight lines with leftover chocolate; leave to set. Pipe melted white chocolate between the dark chocolate outlines for teeth; leave to set.

6 Outline cake with brown decorating gel. Decorate cake with mouth, sunglasses and straight lines.

This wiseguy's bright grin will bring out the party animal in everyone

Diamond Jim

His sensuous curves
are easily achieved with
simple savarin pans

FOR THE CAKE:

340g packet buttercake mix

1 quantity Frosting [page 116]

lemon yellow colouring

35cm round prepared board
   [page 115]

TO DECORATE, YOU WILL NEED:

1 packet Berry Fruits
   Rainbow Roll-Ups

black decorating gel

2 green M&M's

Grease two 22cm savarin pans. Make cake according to directions on packet; divide mixture between prepared pans. Bake in moderate oven about 20 minutes. Stand cakes in pans 5 minutes; turn onto wire racks to cool.

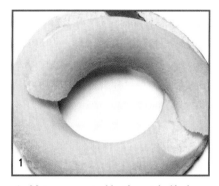

1 Using a serrated knife, cut half of one cake in half at an angle, not cutting through base; reserve cake piece for snake's head.

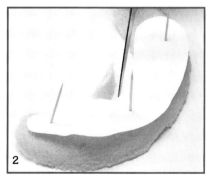

2 Using paper pattern, cut out snake's head from reserved cake piece.

3 Tint Frosting with lemon yellow colouring; spread all cake pieces with Frosting.

4 Assemble cake on board, with the various cake pieces topping one another.

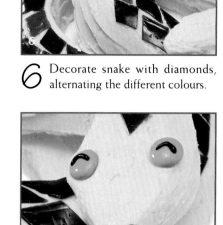

5 Using scissors, cut Roll-ups into even-size diamond shapes.

6 Decorate snake with diamonds, alternating the different colours.

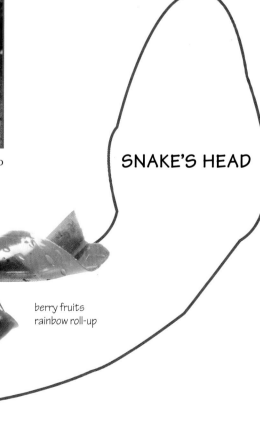

7 Using black decorating gel, make snake-eye slit shapes on M&M's for pupils; position eyes on snake. Place tongue in position. Using piping gel, pipe nostrils and mouth.

SNAKE'S HEAD

berry fruits
rainbow roll-up

Lamington Castle

A palace fit for a king

FOR THE CASTLE:

40cm x 50cm rectangular prepared board [page 115]

6 x 350g packets chocolate finger lamingtons (6.5cm long)

2 quantities chocolate Frosting [page 116]

2 x 350g packet chocolate lamingtons (6.5cm square)

3 x 280g packets pink lamingtons (7cm round)

We used Top Taste chocolate lamingtons and Farmland strawberry lamingtons for this cake.

TO DECORATE, YOU WILL NEED:

4 pink ice-cream wafers

4 wooden skewers

2 cups (300g) dark chocolate Melts, melted

4 ice-cream cones

1 x 20cm long chain

assorted toy soldiers, horses, etc

1 On board, make rectangular base for castle using 4 finger lamingtons for the shorter sides and 5 finger lamingtons for the longer sides; join lamingtons with some of the Frosting. Build a second level on the castle wall in a brickwork pattern, cutting lamingtons to fit. Leave a space on one wall for the doorway. Continue brickwork pattern until 5 layers high.

2 Cut a wafer the width of a finger lamington for support above door; cut 2 wafers for castle doors. Position wafer support over door, secure with Frosting on both sides. Build a sixth layer of castle wall with all but 2 of the remaining finger lamingtons.

3 Position 1 square of chocolate lamington on each of the 4 castle corners; secure with Frosting. Cut 4 square lamingtons in half; position, cut-side down, to form battlements. Cut 2 finger lamingtons into 3 pieces each; place 1 piece in each corner, on top of each of the 4 square lamingtons. Discard remaining 2 finger lamington pieces and remaining square lamingtons.

4 Stack 5 pink lamingtons; push a skewer through centre. Repeat with 15 more pink lamingtons. Position 1 lamington stack at each castle corner.

5 Spread some of the melted chocolate over each ice-cream cone; leave to set. Place a cone on top of each pink lamington stack to form turrets.

6 Trace 6cm x 7cm portcullis shape on baking paper. Pipe melted chocolate over shape; pipe outline around doors and drawbridge. Leave to set.

7 Carefully peel away baking paper from portcullis; position over doorway, secure with Frosting. Secure chain in place with melted chocolate. Position doors and remaining wafer for drawbridge. Arrange toys, etc, as desired.

FOR THE CAKE:

3 x 340g packets buttercake mix

70cm square prepared board [page 115]

3 quantities Frosting [page 116]

green, red and yellow colourings

vegetable oil, for deep-frying

TO DECORATE, YOU WILL NEED:

2 x 200g packets spearmint leaves

3 green musk sticks

2 savoiardi (sponge finger) biscuits

1 red snake

2 strawberries & cream sweets

blue decorating gel

1 black licorice strap

11 sour gummi beans

1 small shell

2 scallop shells

250g bean thread vermicelli

Grease three 20cm x 30cm lamington pans, line bases with baking paper. Using 3 packets, prepare cake mix according to directions; divide among prepared pans. Bake in moderate oven about 25 minutes. Stand cakes in pans 5 minutes; turn onto wire racks to cool.

1 Using paper patterns, cut out tail and body of mermaid from 2 of the cakes.

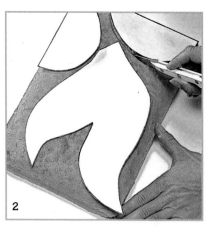

2 Cut out the fin and 2 semi-circles for head from remaining cake.

3 Join cake pieces on board with some of the untinted Frosting.

4 Tint two-thirds of Frosting with green colouring; tint remaining third Frosting to a skin tone using red and yellow colourings.

5 Spread green Frosting over top and side of tail and skin-tone Frosting over top and side of body and head.

6 Cut spearmint leaves lengthways through the centre; cover tail with spearmint leaves. Use green musk sticks to separate tail from body. Position biscuits for arms. Cut mouth from red snake. Make the eyes with strawberries & cream sweets and blue gel; make the eyelashes with strips of licorice; make the necklace with gummi beans and small shell. Decorate cake with shells and sweets as shown. Deep-fry vermicelli in hot oil until puffed; drain on absorbent paper. Shape and style vermicelli hair by cutting and separating noodles; position hair around head.

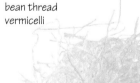

bean thread vermicelli

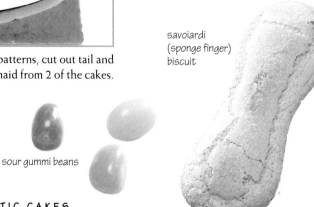

savoiardi (sponge finger) biscuit

sour gummi beans

strawberries & cream sweet

Mindy Mermaid

With Mindy as the star attraction, the party is sure to go swimmingly

Volcano Vibes

A mountain of
fun in an
explosion of
ice-cream,
honeycomb and
rocky road

FOR THE VOLCANO:

4 litres Neapolitan ice-cream

340g packet buttercake mix

3/4 cup (165g) caster sugar

1/4 cup (60ml) water

1 cup (90g) desiccated coconut

green colouring

40cm round prepared board
[page 115]

600ml thickened cream

1/4 cup (25g) cocoa powder

2 tablespoons icing sugar mixture

TO DECORATE, YOU WILL NEED:

4 x 375g packets rocky road,
chopped roughly

4 x 50g Violet Crumble bars,
chopped roughly

1/2 cup (125ml) thick strawberry
topping

5 sparklers

Grease a 20cm Dolly Varden mould
(2.5-litre/10-cup capacity), line with
plastic wrap, extending plastic about 5cm
over edge of mould.

rocky road

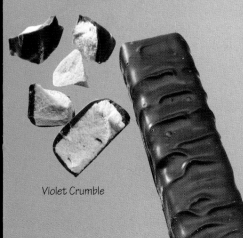
Violet Crumble

1 Separate vanilla, chocolate and
strawberry ice-cream into 3 bowls.
Using a slotted spoon, push down on ice-
cream until just soft. Scoop alternate
spoonfuls of each colour into prepared
mould. Tap mould on bench to settle ice-
cream; cover with foil and freeze overnight. Grease deep 20cm round cake
pan, line base with baking paper. Make
cake according to directions on packet.
Bake in moderate oven about 50 minutes. Stand cake in pan 5 minutes; turn
onto wire rack to cool.

2 Combine sugar and water in small
pan, stir over heat, without boiling,
until sugar dissolves. Boil mixture, uncovered, without stirring, about 10 minutes
or until it becomes a caramel colour.

3 Pour hot toffee onto greased foil-
covered oven tray. Leave to set
then carefully peel away foil and break
toffee into large pieces.

4 Combine coconut and a few drops
of green colouring in a plastic bag;
shake and press bag until coconut is
tinted green.

5 Place cake on board. Beat cream
with sifted cocoa and icing sugar in
medium bowl with electric mixer until
firm peaks form. Spread a quarter of the
cream mixture over top and side of cake.

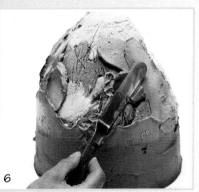

6 Remove ice-cream from mould,
place on cake; spread remaining
cream over the ice-cream. Decorate with
rocky road, Violet Crumble and toffee
pieces. Drizzle volcano with topping.
Sprinkle green coconut around base of
volcano; insert sparklers around the top
of the volcano.

Treasure Chest

Pirates are never out of style, and a chocolate chest overflowing with sweets will be treasured

FOR THE CHEST:

340g packet buttercake mix

4 x 375g packets dark chocolate
 Melts

ICING

2 cups (320g) icing sugar mixture

30g butter, softened

1 tablespoon hot water,
 approximately

35cm x 45cm rectangular
 prepared board [page 115]

TO DECORATE, YOU WILL NEED:

1 x 250g packet M&M's

¼ cup (50g) chocolate sprinkles

black and red decorating gel

assorted lollies

Line 2 x 12-hole muffin pans (⅓-cup/80ml capacity) with paper patty cases. Make cake according to directions on packet. Spoon mixture into cases. Bake in moderate oven about 15 minutes. Stand cakes in pans 5 minutes; turn onto a wire rack to cool.

1 To make Icing, place icing sugar in a medium heatproof bowl; stir in butter and enough water to make a stiff paste. Place bowl over pan of simmering water, stir until icing is spreadable.

2 Spread cakes with Icing, decorate like pirates' faces with M&M's, chocolate sprinkles and decorating gel.

3 Mark two 20cm x 28cm rectangles on separate sheets of baking paper for the base and lid of the treasure chest. Mark 2 more 12cm x 28cm rectangles and 2 more measuring 12cm x 20cm for sides.

4 Melt 500g of the dark chocolate; spread chocolate evenly over base and lid patterns, draping lid sheet over a large cylindrical shape (like a jar on its side). Leave to set then trim edges, reserving any leftover chocolate.

Melt another 250g of dark chocolate; spread evenly over the patterns for the 2 short sides of the chest. Leave to set then trim edges, reserving any leftover chocolate. Melt another 400g of the dark chocolate; spread chocolate evenly over the patterns for the 2 long sides of the chest. Leave to set, trim edges, reserving any leftover chocolate.

5 To assemble chest on board, melt remaining dark chocolate with reserved scraps of chocolate. Working with two pieces at a time, brush the edges to be joined with chocolate and press together, supporting sides with tumblers until set.

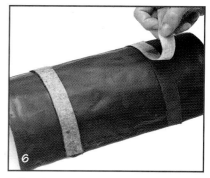

6 Cut strips of baking paper about 2cm wide and long enough to go around the chest's lid and sides twice; spread with remaining melted chocolate. Working quickly, place strips over lid and on sides into position as shown. When chocolate is set, peel away paper.

7 Outline chocolate "bands" on chest with black decorating gel; pipe dots to resemble "rivets" holding bands onto chest. Fill chest with pirate cakes and assorted lollies. Place lid in position.

FOR THE CAKE:

2 x 340g packets buttercake mix

2 x 500g packets ready-made icing

icing sugar mixture

pink colouring

35cm square prepared board [page 115]

½ cup (125ml) apricot jam, warmed, strained

TO DECORATE, YOU WILL NEED:

1 non-toxic felt-tip pen

heart-shaped cutter

1m x 5cm purple ribbon

1m x 2.5cm purple ribbon

assorted fresh or silk flowers

Grease deep 23cm square cake pan, line base with baking paper. Using 2 packets, prepare cake mix according to directions; pour into prepared pan. Bake in moderate oven about 1 hour. Stand cake in pan for 5 minutes; turn onto wire rack to cool. Using a serrated knife, level top of cake.

1 On a surface dusted with icing sugar, knead icing until smooth. Reserve 1 tablespoon white icing for message tag. Knead colouring into remaining icing.

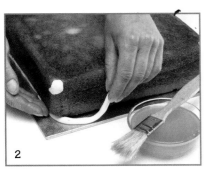

2 Place cake, base-side up, on board. Patch top, sides and base of cake with a little of the icing. Brush top and sides of cake evenly with some of the jam.

3 Divide pink icing in half, wrap one half tightly in plastic wrap. On a surface dusted with icing sugar, roll out other half of icing until large enough to cover top and sides of cake. Lift icing over cake then mould icing onto cake with hands dusted with icing sugar; trim edges of cake neatly. Brush top and sides of cake with more jam. Repeat process with remaining half of the pink icing.

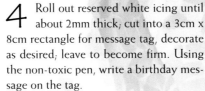

4 Roll out reserved white icing until about 2mm thick; cut into a 3cm x 8cm rectangle for message tag, decorate as desired; leave to become firm. Using the non-toxic pen, write a birthday message on the tag.

5 Gently press a small heart-shaped cutter into icing all around cake. Position ribbons as for a present, tucking ends under cake. Decorate top of cake with flowers and tag.

Surprise Package

*Dress up your cake with this
pretty gift-wrap idea*

Edward Bear

FOR THE CAKE:

4 x 340g packets buttercake mix

35cm x 60cm rectangular prepared board [page 115]

3 quantities Frosting [page 116]

brown, red and ivory colourings

TO DECORATE, YOU WILL NEED:

1 milk chocolate Melt

2 brown Smarties

2 small red foil-covered chocolate hearts

about 17 red Smarties

75cm thin red licorice rope

35g jar green snowflakes

Grease 2 deep 25cm round cake pans, line bases with baking paper. Using 4 packets, prepare cake mix according to directions; divide between prepared pans. Bake in moderate oven for about 1 hour. Stand cakes in pans 5 minutes; turn onto wire racks to cool.

1 Using paper pattern, cut out bear's face and paws from 1 cake.

2 Cut paws in half, then slice at an angle as shown.

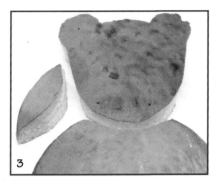

3 Cut a rounded shape out of remaining cake where head joins body. Position head, body and paws on board.

4 Tint one-third of the Frosting light brown. Divide remaining Frosting into 3 portions: tint 1 portion dark brown; another portion red; and remaining Frosting ivory.

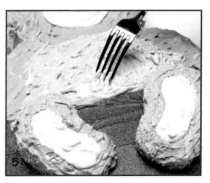

5 Using a small sharp knife, mark out trouser line on cake. Spread top and side of cake with Frostings, making nose and belly slightly rounded, and blending in ivory Frosting. Spread paws with Frosting, position on cake. Run a fork through brown Frosting to give a textured effect.

6 Cut 1 milk chocolate Melt into a triangle, place on face for nose. Position brown Smarties for eyes. Position chocolate hearts and a red Smartie for bow-tie. Make braces from red licorice rope; position Smarties in between each pair of licorice rope. Place snowflakes on trousers. Spoon dark brown Frosting into a piping bag fitted with a small plain tube; pipe mouth and front paws. Run a fork gently run through Frosting on paws to give a textured effect.

It's always a picnic when Teddy comes to the party

green snowflakes

small red foil-covered chocolate heart

Rad Dog

A radical character if ever there was one

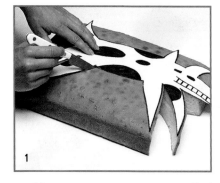

1 Using paper pattern, cut out Rad Dog; reserve leftover cake.

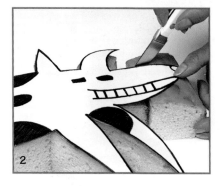

2 Position leftover cake at head end to complete nose. Use paper pattern to cut out nose. Place cake on board. Join nose to cake and secure with a little orange Frosting.

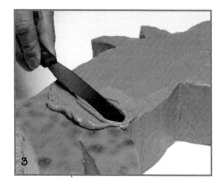

3 Tint two-thirds of the Frosting with orange colouring; tint remaining one-third Frosting with blue colouring. Spread top and side of cake with orange Frosting.

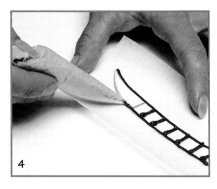

4 Trace outline of Rad Dog's mouth on baking paper. Turn paper over so outline is underneath. Pipe melted dark chocolate over traced lines to form mouth and teeth; leave to set.

FOR THE CAKE:

3 x 340g packets buttercake mix

40cm x 50cm rectangular prepared board [page 115]

2 quantities Frosting [page 116]

orange and blue colourings

TO DECORATE, YOU WILL NEED:

⅓ cup (50g) dark chocolate Melts, melted

⅓ cup (50g) white chocolate Melts, melted

2 chocolate bullets

3 Jaffas

80cm green Fruity Metres

40cm red Fruity Metres

2 black licorice straps

20 silver cachous

Grease 26cm x 36cm baking dish [base measurements], line base with baking paper. Using 3 packets, prepare cake mix according to directions; pour into prepared dish. Bake in moderate oven about 1 hour. Stand cake in the dish for 5 minutes; turn onto wire rack to cool.

5 Pipe melted white chocolate onto teeth, as shown; leave to set. Carefully peel mouth off baking paper and position on dog's face.

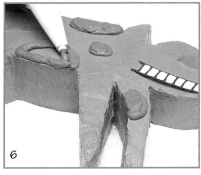

6 Spoon blue Frosting into piping bag fitted with a small plain tube; pipe spots onto dog. Position bullets for eyes and a Jaffa for the nose.

7 To make skateboard, place Fruity Metres on bench, overlapping the edges slightly; trim to form skateboard. Cut one licorice strap in half lengthways; wrap one piece around a Jaffa, continuing with second half; secure with a little Frosting. Position 10 silver cachous as shown; place wheel under skateboard. Repeat with the remaining licorice strap, Jaffa and cachous.

FOR THE CAKE:

3 x 340g packets buttercake mix

40cm square prepared board [page 115]

2 quantities Frosting [page 116]

violet, yellow, pink, green and blue colourings

TO DECORATE, YOU WILL NEED:

about 34 pink Smarties

about 26 blue Smarties

35g jar snowflakes

1 mauve pipe cleaner

2 lollipops

Grease deep 30cm square cake pan, line base with baking paper. Using 3 packets, prepare cake mix according to directions; pour into prepared pan. Bake in moderate oven about 1¼ hours. Stand cake in pan 10 minutes; turn onto wire rack to cool.

1 Using paper pattern, cut out the butterfly. Place cake on board.

2 Tint one-third of the Frosting with violet colouring, and another third with yellow colouring. Divide the remaining Frosting among 3 bowls. Tint one portion with pink colouring, one with green colouring and one with blue.

3 Following outlines on the pattern, spread Frosting on cake.

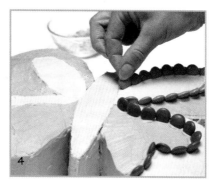

4 Position Smarties around edges of different Frosting colours; dot all over with snowflakes. Twist pipe cleaner to resemble antennae; position pipe cleaner and lollipops as shown.

lollipops

snowflakes

The glittering wings will bring a flutter to the eyes of your little girl

Butterfly Beauty

The Yummy Yoyo

FOR THE CAKE:

2 x 340g packets buttercake mix

2 quantities Frosting [page 116]

green, red, blue and yellow
   colourings

35cm round prepared board
   [page 115]

TO DECORATE, YOU WILL NEED:

thin red licorice rope

Grease 2 deep 22cm round cake pans,
line bases and sides with baking paper.
Using both packets, prepare cake mix
according to directions; divide between
prepared pans. Bake in moderate oven
about 40 minutes. Stand cakes in pans
5 minutes; turn onto wire racks to cool.

1 Using a sharp knife, trim about 1cm diagonally off the base edge of both the cakes.

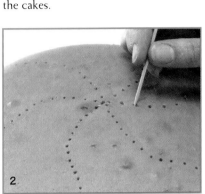

2 Using a toothpick or skewer, mark top and side of each cake into 6 equal size swirl-shape segments.

3 Divide Frosting equally in 4 portions; tint one portion with red colouring, another with blue, the third with yellow, and the fourth one green.

4 Place one of the cakes, base-side up, on board. Sandwich the cakes, bases together, with green Frosting.

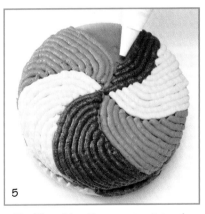

5 Place blue Frosting in piping bag fitted with a small plain tube; pipe into 2 opposing swirl-shape segments. Repeat with yellow and red Frostings. Knot one end of red licorice rope together and twist rope to make the Yoyo string.

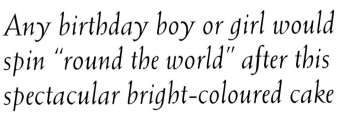

Any birthday boy or girl would spin "round the world" after this spectacular bright-coloured cake

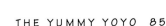

Ice-cream and tinted chocolate make up the fairytale dress fit for a Princess

FOR THE PRINCESS:

4 litres Neapolitan ice-cream

1¹/2 cups (225g) white chocolate Melts, melted

pink and blue colourings

40cm round prepared board [page 115]

TO DECORATE, YOU WILL NEED:

1 small doll

pink and gold hair mascara

silver cardboard

1 pink and 1 purple pipe-cleaner

2m x 5cm pink organza ribbon

2m x 5cm blue organza ribbon

Grease a 20cm Dolly Varden mould (2.5-litre/10-cup capacity), line with plastic wrap, extending plastic about 5cm over edge of mould.

1 Separate vanilla, strawberry and chocolate ice-cream into 3 bowls. Using a slotted spoon, press down on ice-cream until just soft. Scoop alternate spoonfuls of each colour into mould. Tap mould on bench to settle ice-cream; cover with foil, freeze overnight.

2 Remove legs from doll, colour hair with mascara. Separate the melted chocolate into 2 bowls; tint half the chocolate with pink colouring and half with blue. Using a spoon, coat bodice area of the doll's body with some of the pink chocolate. Tap doll on the bench to smooth out chocolate; leave to set.

3 Trace outline of wings on baking paper. Turn paper over so outline is underneath. Pipe pink chocolate over traced lines to form wings and hearts; leave to set.

4 Pipe blue chocolate in a scrolled pattern inside wings; leave to set. Pipe a little of the remaining blue chocolate in a decorative pattern onto the doll's pink bodice.

5 Carefully peel the wings from the baking paper. Supporting wings between 2 bowls, join them together with pink chocolate; leave to set.

6 To make wand, cut 2 small stars out of the silver cardboard. Cut pink pipe-cleaner 10cm long; fix 1 end between the stars. Using purple pipe-cleaner, make a crown; secure around the doll's head.

7 Remove ice-cream from mould; place on board. Using a teaspoon, scoop out a small hole in the top of ice-cream; secure doll in hole with a little melted chocolate. Drizzle pink and blue chocolate over ice-cream in a decorative pattern to make doll's skirt; return to freezer until set. Tie ribbon into a bow around doll's waist. Attach wings to doll's back with a little chocolate; return to freezer until required.

Fairy Princess

FOR THE CAKE:

2 x 340g packets buttercake mix

3 cups (450g) white chocolate Melts, melted

blue colouring

1/4 cup (60ml) light corn syrup

35cm x 40cm rectangular prepared board [page 115]

1/4 cup (60ml) apricot jam, warmed, sieved

icing sugar mixture

TO DECORATE, YOU WILL NEED:

3 x 60cm pieces thin red licorice rope

gum balls of assorted sizes and colours

black decorating gel

Grease deep 25cm round cake pan, line base with baking paper. Using both packets, prepare cake mix according to directions; pour into prepared pan. Bake in moderate oven about 1 hour. Stand cake in pan for 5 minutes; turn onto wire rack to cool.

1 Tint melted chocolate with blue colouring; add corn syrup, stir until mixture thickens and becomes slightly grainy. Cover; stand at room temperature about 1 hour or until mixture is firm.

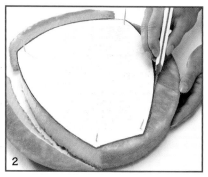

2 Using paper pattern, cut out the marble bag. Place cake, base-side up, on the board.

3 Using a sharp knife, slightly trim top of cake at an angle towards "opening" of the marble bag. Brush top and sides of cake evenly with warm jam.

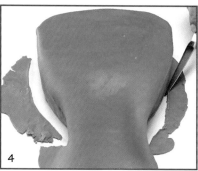

4 On a surface dusted with icing sugar, knead blue chocolate mixture until smooth and soft. Roll out on a sheet of baking paper until large enough to cover top and side of cake. Carefully place chocolate on cake, press firmly around side of cake, trim around edge (except for the bag's opening); reserve any leftover chocolate mixture.

5 Gently ease the chocolate mixture around the bag's opening into decorative folds. Re-roll reserved excess chocolate mixture; place in folds around opening to make a double layer, trim to neaten edges. Roll a sausage shape about 10cm long from chocolate trimmings; press over joins of decorative folds.

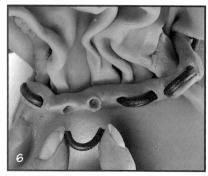

6 Using a skewer or toothpick, pierce holes about 1.5cm apart on the bag's opening; press short pieces of licorice into holes to look like stitched-in drawstring. Bend 2 x 60cm pieces of licorice in half and attach to side of opening to resemble the pulls on drawstrings. Place the gum balls in position and pipe a message on the bag with decorating gel.

Marble Bag

The birthday guests will all lose their marbles over this ingenious bag of tricks

Kindy Blocks

As simple as A-B-C, you can count on the nursery set adoring these cakes

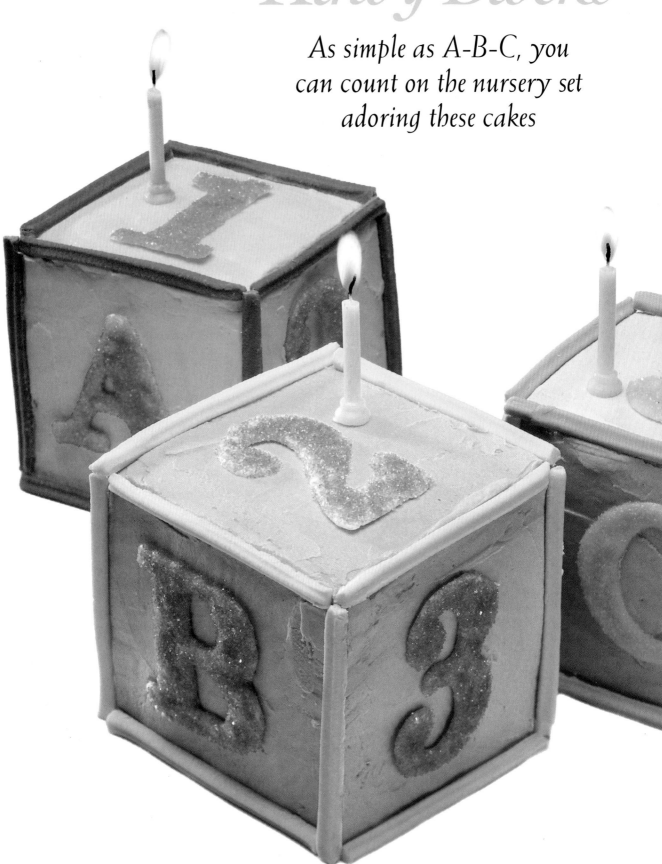

FOR THE CAKE:

4 x 340g packets buttercake mix

3 quantities Frosting [page 116]

pink, sky blue and yellow colourings

35cm square prepared board
   [page 115]

TO DECORATE, YOU WILL NEED:

3 yellow musk sticks

3 pink musk sticks

3 green musk sticks

3/4 cup (105g) white chocolate
   Melts, melted

yellow, blue and pink sugar crystals

Grease 2 deep 23cm square cake pans, line bases with baking paper. Using the 4 packets, prepare cake mix according to directions; divide between prepared pans. Bake in moderate oven for about 1 hour. Stand cakes in pans 5 minutes; turn onto wire racks to cool.

1 Using a serrated knife, level tops of cakes so that one is 5cm high and the other cake is 6cm high. Cut each cake into 4 squares.

2 Tint one-third of the Frosting with pink colouring, another third with blue and the remainder with yellow.

3 Sandwich a 5cm- and 6cm-high square with some Frosting. Repeat until you have 3 x 11cm cubes. (There will be one piece of each thickness of cake left over.) Spread each block with a different colour Frosting. Arrange the blocks on the board.

4 Cut each musk stick lengthways into 4 even-size strips; outline all edges of blocks with musk sticks.

5 Pipe melted chocolate numbers and letters on baking paper.

6 Before chocolate sets, sprinkle with sugar crystals; leave to set. Carefully peel numbers and letters off baking paper and position on blocks.

Silly Tilly

Who could resist Tilly with her yummy chocolate shell?

FOR THE CAKE:

3 x 340g packets buttercake mix

35cm x 45cm rectangular
prepared board [page 115]

300ml thickened cream

½ cup (125ml) strawberry jam

2 quantities Frosting [page 116]

green, pink and red colourings

1 cup (150g) white chocolate
Melts, melted

TO DECORATE, YOU WILL NEED:

1 white marshmallow

blue and black decorating gel

thin red licorice rope

Grease 26cm x 32cm baking dish (base
measurements), line base with baking
paper. Using 3 packets, prepare cake mix
according to directions; pour into prepared dish. Bake in moderate oven about
45 minutes. Stand cake in dish 5 minutes;
turn onto wire rack to cool.

1 Using paper pattern, cut out Tilly's
body and the single flipper as shown;
reserve leftover cake pieces. Place cake
on the board.

2 Beat cream in small bowl with
electric mixer until soft peaks form.
Chop reserved leftover cake into 2cm
pieces; fold cake pieces and jam into
cream. Spoon cream mixture on top of
cake to form the dome of Tilly's back.

3 Divide Frosting between 2 bowls;
tint half of the Frosting dark green
and the other half light green. Spread top
of the cake and cream mixture with light
green Frosting; spread the dark green
Frosting around feet, flippers, head and
side of cake.

4 Hand-draw an approximate-size
outline of Tilly's back on baking
paper; turn paper over. Divide the melted
chocolate between 2 bowls; tint half of
the chocolate with pink colouring and
the other half red. Pour both tinted
chocolates, in patches, onto baking
paper within the marks of the outline.
Using a toothpick or skewer, swirl the
chocolate patches together, marbling the
pink and red into a tortoise-shell pattern.
Leave to set; break into pieces.

5 Press chocolate pieces onto Tilly's
back, as shown.

6 To make eyes, cut marshmallow in
half; pipe dots with blue and black
gel to complete eyes, position on head.
Use red licorice to create mouth. Pipe
wavy lines on board with blue gel to
represent flowing water.

Packaged pavlova shells are available from most supermarkets. Use flowers of your choice if lisianthus and tuberoses are not in season. Parafilm tape, used in floral arrangements, is available from florists or specialty stores.

FOR THE CAKE:

3 x 500g purchased pavlova shells

35cm round prepared board [page 115]

600ml thickened cream

2 tablespoons icing sugar mixture

TO DECORATE, YOU WILL NEED:

200g large pink and white marshmallows

1 cup (70g) shredded coconut

8 pink lisianthus

8 white lisianthus

8 tuberoses

parafilm tape

silver cachous

1m pink organza ribbon

1m silver organza ribbon

2 Beat cream and icing sugar in medium bowl with electric mixer until soft peaks form. Spread cream over top of crushed pavlovas.

3 Press marshmallows into cream; sprinkle with coconut.

A flounce of pastel flowers makes this extravagant bouquet

1 Place 1 pavlova shell on board. Crush remaining 2 pavlova shells; pile over top to form a dome.

4 Shorten flower stems to about 5cm in length; wrap stems with tape. Position flowers in between marshmallows all over cake. Dust cake with a little sifted icing sugar; scatter silver cachous over cake. Tie 1 ribbon into a bow; tie the remaining ribbon around base of the cake, attach the bow to the front.

Flower Bombe

Clowning Around

FOR THE CAKE:

3 x 340g packets buttercake mix

2 quantities Frosting [page 116]

red, green, blue and yellow
    colourings

30cm x 60cm rectangular
    prepared board [page 115]

TO DECORATE, YOU WILL NEED:

100g packet Chang's fried noodles

1 black licorice strap

thin red licorice rope

1 large red gum ball

1 large yellow gum ball

11 small gum balls in
    assorted colours

Grease deep 19cm square and deep 22cm round cake pans; line bases with baking paper. Using 3 packets, prepare cake mix according to directions; divide between prepared pans. Bake cakes in moderate oven about 1 hour. Stand cakes in pans 5 minutes; turn onto wire racks to cool.

Everyone loves a clown and this winning face is sure to charm the partygoers

1   Place half of the Frosting, untinted, in a medium bowl; reserve. Place 2 tablespoons of the remaining Frosting in a small bowl; tint with red colouring. Divide remaining Frosting into 2 small bowls; tint one portion with green colouring and the other with blue.

2   If necessary, level tops of cakes so they are of the same height, using a serrated knife. Mark halfway point on top edge of square cake; cut from halfway point to bottom corners to form a large triangle for hat. Cut 2 even-sided triangles from remaining corners of square cake; there will be leftover cake.

3   Place round cake, base-side up, on board; position the cake triangles as shown.

4   Spread clown with white, green and blue Frosting.

5   Place noodles in small plastic bag with a few drops of yellow colouring; shake well. When noodles are dry, place around face for hair.

6   Cut small pieces of licorice for each eye and eyebrow; place in position. Outline smile with red licorice; spread red Frosting inside smile, repeat for cheeks. Place a small half-circle of black licorice inside smile. Position large gum balls for nose and bow-tie "knot"; place the smaller gum balls on the hat. Outline bow-tie with red licorice; make a 3-petalled daisy at top of hat with red licorice and a gum ball.

Bush Babies

FOR THE CAKE:

2 x 340g packets buttercake mix

30cm round prepared board
   [page 115]

1½ quantities chocolate Frosting
   [page 116]

icing sugar mixture

500g packet ready-made icing

juniper green, kelly green, willow
   green, brown and black food
   colourings

TO DECORATE, YOU WILL NEED:

white and pink decorating gel

non-toxic black felt-tipped pen

60cm x 3.5cm sheer gold ribbon

Grease deep 22cm round cake pan, line base with baking paper. Using 2 packets, prepare cakes according to directions; pour into prepared pan. Bake in moderate oven about 1 hour. Stand cake in pan for 5 minutes; turn onto wire rack to cool.

1 Using a serrated knife, level top of cake. Place cake, base-side up, on board; spread top and side with Frosting.

2 On a surface dusted with icing sugar, knead icing until smooth and pliable. Divide icing into thirds; cover two-thirds of the icing with plastic wrap, pressing plastic down firmly onto the surface of the icing to prevent it drying out, reserve. Tint one quarter of the remaining icing with juniper green colouring; tint half of the remaining icing with willow green colouring; tint the rest with kelly green colouring. Knead half of the willow green icing and half of the kelly green icing together to make a fourth green colour. Wrap each ball of icing individually in plastic wrap to prevent them drying out.

3 On a surface dusted with icing sugar, roll out the 4 individual icing balls about 2mm thick. Using a small sharp knife, cut out gum leaf shapes; reroll icing scraps to cut out more gum leaf shapes. Twist leaves slightly; drape over edge of pan to dry.

4 On a surface dusted with icing sugar, tint half of the reserved two-thirds of the icing a wombat colour with brown colouring; tint the remaining half a grey koala colour using the black colouring. Cut off about a third of each of the 2 colours; knead together to make a third grey-brown possum colour.

5 Divide the brown icing in half, reserving a little to make the wombats' noses. Shape 2 wombat bodies; make a small cut under each chin, pinch together to shape each head. Pinch sides of head to make ears; use a skewer to make eyes. Divide grey icing into quarters, reserving a little to make the koalas' eyes and noses. Shape 2 koala bodies and 2 heads; attach heads to bodies using a little water. Divide grey-brown colour into quarters, reserving a little to make possums' eyes and noses. Shape 2 possum bodies and 2 heads; attach heads to bodies using a little water.

6 Finish animals by rolling reserved 3 colours of icing into tiny balls for eyes and noses; attach using a little water. Use a skewer to make pupils for eyes, nostrils and mouths. Colour wombats' and koalas' noses with non-toxic black pen; colour possums' noses with pink decorating gel; colour fur on koalas' ears with white decorating gel. Arrange leaves on top of the cake; place animals on top of leaves. Wrap ribbon around side of cake, tie into bow.

It's easy to make an authentically Australian menagerie – hide them in a deluge of fallen gum leaves

FOR THE CAKE:

3 x 340g packets buttercake mix

35cm x 45cm rectangular prepared board [page 115]

2 quantities Frosting [page 116]

black colouring

TO DECORATE, YOU WILL NEED:

3 marshmallows

2 black licorice straps

pink and black decorating gel

2 green M&M's

2 white chocolate Melts

1 x 140g packet thin red licorice rope

Grease 26cm x 36cm baking dish (base measurements), line base with baking paper. Using 3 packets, prepare cake mix according to directions; pour into prepared dish. Bake in moderate oven about 1 hour. Stand cake in dish for 5 minutes; turn onto wire rack to cool.

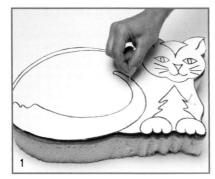

1 Using paper pattern, cut out cat. Place cake on board. Mark out head and tail with toothpick or skewer.

2 Cut 1 marshmallow into 4 pieces; position on face for cheeks, chin and nose. Place 1 marshmallow on each paw.

Darling Dudley

If the birthday person is mad about cats, this enigmatic creation will be ... Purrfection

3 Reserve one-quarter of the Frosting. Tint remaining Frosting grey with black colouring.

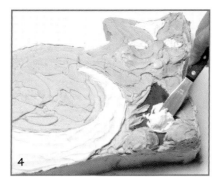

4 Spread body with grey Frosting. Spread head marking, eyes, chest and stripe with white Frosting.

5 Dot tail with grey Frosting to make stripes. Using fork, blend Frosting on back and tail stripes; fluff Frosting with a fork to resemble fur.

6 Cut 1 licorice strap into thin strips; outline body, tail, head, ears, eyes and paws with licorice. Pipe nose with pink decorating gel. Pipe mouth with black gel. Cut remaining licorice into 6 x 3cm strips; attach for whiskers. Press M&M's into Frosting for eyes; mark pupils with black decorating gel. Cut white chocolate Melts into quarters, use 3 pieces for claws on each paw. Roll the licorice rope into a "ball of yarn", and stick 2 skewers or chopsticks into it, if desired.

Canada

Great Britain

Waving the Flag

Strike a patriotic note with one of these berry imaginative creations

FOR THE CAKES:

The quantities given for cake, cream and berries are enough to make one Flag Cake.

3 x 340g packets buttercake mix

600ml thickened cream

35cm x 45cm rectangular prepared board [page 115]

TO DECORATE, YOU WILL NEED:

AUSTRALIAN FLAG

500g strawberries

1.5kg blueberries

1 cup (150g) white chocolate Melts, melted

BRITISH FLAG

1.25kg strawberries

750g blueberries

CANADIAN FLAG

1.5kg strawberries

Grease 26cm x 36cm baking dish (base measurements), line base with baking paper. Using 3 packets, prepare cake mix according to directions; pour into prepared dish. Bake in moderate oven about 1 hour. Stand cake in dish for 5 minutes; turn onto wire rack to cool. Place cake, base-side up, on board.

Beat cream in medium bowl with electric mixer until soft peaks form. Spread cake with cream. Place berries on cake for desired flag, as shown, trimming and slicing the strawberries where necessary. For the Australian Flag cake, place white chocolate stars (see below) on top to form the Southern Cross.

To make the chocolate stars, spread melted white chocolate on a sheet of baking paper. When chocolate is almost set, cut out stars with a knife.

Australia

Footy Fever

A cake in the shape of a football jersey. Decorate it with the colours of your child's favourite team to make him the hero of the day

FOR THE CAKE:

4 x 340g packets buttercake mix

40cm x 60cm rectangular prepared board [page 115]

2 quantities Frosting [page 116]

yellow and blue colourings

2/3 cup (100g) white chocolate Melts, melted

TO DECORATE, YOU WILL NEED:

130g tube red Fruity Metres

130g tube green Fruity Metres

black decorating gel

blue and yellow candy letter decorations

Grease two 26cm x 32cm baking dishes (base measurements), line bases with baking paper. Using 4 packets, prepare cake mix according to directions; divide mixture evenly among prepared dishes. Bake in moderate oven about 35 minutes. Stand cake in dishes 5 minutes; turn onto wire rack to cool.

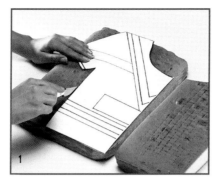

1 Using paper pattern, cut out half the jersey, turn pattern over and cut out other half. Place cakes on board.

3 Cut and position red and green Fruity Metres as shown.

2 Tint Frosting with yellow colouring. Spread top and side of the cake with Frosting.

4 To make Happy Birthday and number plaques, make outlines of a 4cm x 16cm rectangle and 5.5cm circle on baking paper. Tint melted chocolate with blue colouring. Spread chocolate within the rectangle and circle outlines; when chocolate is almost set, trim edges; peel off paper.

5 Using decorating gel, pipe on plaques. Carefully lift and position plaques on cake. Press candy letters onto sleeves of jersey, as desired.

blue and yellow candy letter decorations

We've selected these 2 balls as random examples; use the directions as a guide to make your child's favourite sport equipment.

FOR THE CAKE:

3 x 340g packets buttercake mix

30cm round prepared board [page 115]

2 quantities Frosting [page 116]

TO DECORATE, YOU WILL NEED:

1¹/3 cups (200g) dark chocolate Melts, melted

1 black licorice strap

Grease 2 large 2.25-litre (9-cup) capacity pudding steamers. Using 3 packets, prepare cake mix according to directions; pour into prepared steamers. Bake in moderate oven about 1 hour. Stand cakes in steamers 5 minutes; turn onto wire racks to cool.

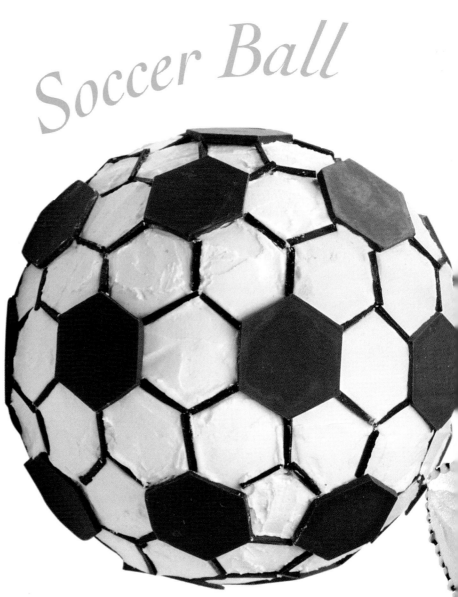

Soccer Ball

1 Using a serrated knife, level tops of cakes; sandwich together on board with Frosting. Spread the cake with the remaining Frosting.

SOCCER PATTERN

2 Spread melted chocolate about 2mm thick on baking paper. Using the paper pattern supplied, left, cut out chocolate hexagons.

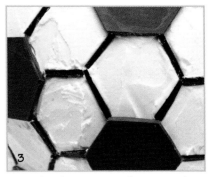

3 Cut licorice into thin 2.5cm long strips. Place chocolate hexagons, base-side up, and licorice strips, in hexagonal patterns, all over cake.

FOR THE CAKE:

3 x 340g packets buttercake mix

2 quantities Frosting [page 116]

30cm x 40cm rectangular prepared board [page 115]

TO DECORATE, YOU WILL NEED:

black and white decorating gel

green and yellow Fruity Metres

thin red licorice rope

½ cup (100g) chocolate thins

Grease two 20cm Dolly Varden moulds (2.5-litre/10-cup capacity). Make cakes according to directions on packets; pour into prepared moulds. Bake in moderate oven 1¼ hours. Stand cakes 5 minutes; turn onto wire racks to cool.

1 Using a serrated knife, level tops of cakes; cut a small section off a side of one cake to give a level base. Securing with a long skewer, sandwich cakes together with Frosting on board. Cover cake with Frosting.

2 Using black decorating gel, mark lines along length of ball; mark out an oval on top of cake. Use white decorating gel to indicate stitches.

3 Using Fruity Metres, make a green and yellow crest. Using black decorating gel, pipe desired message on crest. Position crest on side of ball.

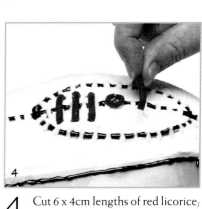

4 Cut 6 x 4cm lengths of red licorice; bend licorice pieces into "laces" and position on top of cake. Make a small pump hole with licorice and position on cake. Sprinkle chocolate thins around base of ball.

Football

Cricket Pitch

The sports fields shown, with appropriately different decorations, could easily become the grounds of your child's favourite sport.

FOR THE CRICKET PITCH CAKE:

3 x 340g packets buttercake mix

1 quantity Frosting [page 116]

green, red and blue colourings

40cm x 45cm rectangular prepared board [page 115]

TO DECORATE, YOU WILL NEED:

¹/3 cup (65g) green sugar crystals

3 teaspoons yellow jelly crystals

toy cricket players and stumps

Grease deep 31cm oval cake pan; line base with baking paper. Using 3 packets, prepare cake mix according to directions; pour into prepared pan. Bake in moderate oven about 1¹/2 hours. Stand cake in pan 5 minutes; turn onto wire rack to cool. Using a serrated knife, level top of cake.

2 Place cake, base-side up, on board. Spread top and side of cake with Frosting; sprinkle top of cake with green sugar crystals.

3 Cut a 4cm x 15cm rectangle out of a piece of cardboard. Place cardboard on cake, sprinkle yellow jelly crystals inside piece of cardboard. Gently lift cardboard off cake. Position players and stumps on cake.

1 Tint Frosting with green colouring, then carefully add a few drops of red and blue colourings, to result in a rich, deep green colour.

Tennis Court

FOR THE TENNIS COURT CAKE:

3 x 340g packets buttercake mix

1 quantity Frosting [page 116]

500g packet ready-made icing

caramel, terracotta, brown and royal blue colourings

35cm x 45cm rectangular prepared board [page 115]

icing sugar mixture

TO DECORATE, YOU WILL NEED:

2m x 2mm wide white ribbon

1 egg white

20cm netting

6 toothpicks

1/2 cup (70g) white chocolate Melts, melted

3 x black licorice straps

2 pieces thin red licorice rope

1/4 cup (35g) dark chocolate Melts, melted

30cm strip strawberry flavoured Fruity Metres

4 small mints

Grease 26cm x 36cm baking dish (base measurements), line base with baking paper. Using 3 packets, prepare cake mix according to directions; pour into prepared dish. Bake in moderate oven about 1 hour. Stand cake in dish for 5 minutes; turn onto wire rack to cool.

1 Tint Frosting with caramel, terracotta and brown colourings. Place cake, base-side up, on prepared board; spread cake with Frosting.

2 On a surface dusted with icing sugar, knead icing until smooth and pliable. Tint icing with blue colouring; knead until colour is evenly distributed. Wrap tightly in plastic; stand until firm, 1 hour or overnight.

3 On a sheet of baking paper dusted with icing sugar, roll out icing evenly to a piece large enough in area to cut out a 15cm x 32.5cm rectangle. Carefully place icing on centre of cake. Cut ribbon into 4 x 32.5cm, 2 x 11.6cm, 2 x 15cm and 1 x 17.4cm lengths. Brush backs of ribbons lightly with egg white; press onto court as shown. Secure net onto cake with toothpicks. To make the Happy Birthday signs, pipe melted chocolate on 10cm pieces of black licorice. Join 2 pieces of licorice together with chocolate and outline with red rope licorice. Position on cake. To make umpire's chair, cut two x 2cm pieces of licorice strap. On each corner of 1 piece of licorice, attach 4 toothpicks. Push 2 toothpicks through licorice and attach the other piece of licorice. Position the chair on the cake.

4 Draw 4 tennis racquets on paper and pipe melted dark chocolate to fill in outline. Pipe racquet strings with melted white chocolate. When set, peel off paper and wrap narrow strips of Fruity Metres around racquet handles. Position on cake along with small mints for balls.

Fields of Play

We've included these diagrams to help start you on your way to achieving the look of your child's favourite playing field, but feel free to lash out with your own embellishments—after all, the only limits imposed on creating a personalised Fantastic Cake are those set by your imagination

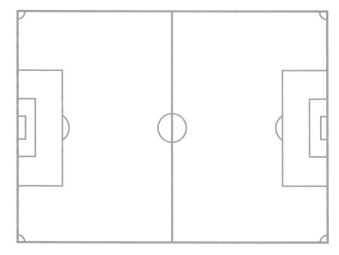

RUGBY LEAGUE

We covered the top of this cake with green sprinkles and sugar crystals, piped the in-goal areas and metre-lines with white decorating icing, made goal posts out of Fruity Metres wrapped around lollipop sticks, and piped the numbers with melted white chocolate.

SOCCER

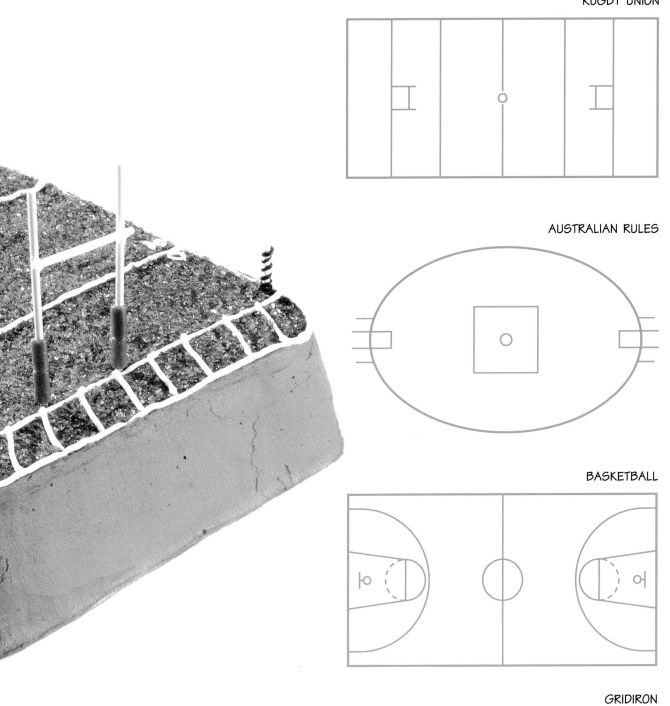

RUGBY UNION

AUSTRALIAN RULES

BASKETBALL

GRIDIRON

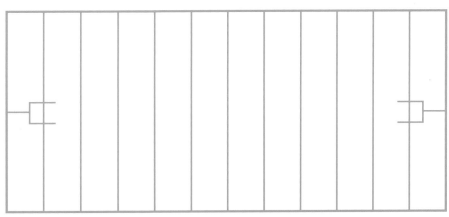

Recipes that Take the Cake

We used packet cake mixes for the majority of our Fantastic Cakes, to ensure consistency of size and texture throughout the book. However, if you would prefer to make your own cake, here are four fabulously easy and delicious suggestions to use as your starting point

Each of these recipes makes a cake equal in quantity to one 340g packet of White Wings Golden Buttercake Cake Mix. Therefore, if the particular Fantastic Cake recipe you have decided to make uses 2 packages of buttercake mix, double the quantities called for in the recipe you've selected and adjust the cooking time accordingly, by referring to the chart on the opposite page.

Basic Butter Cake
[baked in a 12-hole muffin pan]

To make a marble cake, see the main photograph on page 114: place portions of cake mixture in different bowls; tint each with desired colour. Spoon dollops of mixture into prepared pan, alternating colours, then gently swirl together with a skewer or spoon.

125g soft butter

1 teaspoon vanilla essence

3/4 cup (165g) caster sugar

2 eggs

1 1/2 cups (225g) self-raising flour

1/2 cup (125ml) milk

Cream butter, essence and sugar in small bowl with electric mixer until light and fluffy. Beat in eggs, one at time, until combined. Stir in flour and milk, in 2 batches. Spread mixture into prepared pan. Bake in moderate oven until cake is cooked when tested. Stand cake 5 minutes; turn onto wire rack to cool.

Rich Chocolate Cake
[baked in a deep 19cm square pan]

125g soft butter

1 teaspoon vanilla essence

1 1/4 cups (275g) caster sugar

2 eggs

1 1/3 cups (200g) self-raising flour

1/2 cup (50g) cocoa powder

2/3 cup (160ml) water

Combine all ingredients in large bowl; beat on low speed with electric mixer until ingredients are combined. Increase speed to medium, beat about 3 minutes or until mixture is smooth and changed to a lighter colour. Spread into prepared pan. Bake in moderate oven until cake is cooked when tested. Stand cake for 5 minutes; turn onto wire rack to cool.

Best-Ever Sponge
[baked in a deep 20cm round pan]

This recipe does not contain any liquid. For best results, the eggs should be at room temperature.

3 eggs

1/2 cup (110g) caster sugar

1/4 cup (35g) cornflour

1/4 cup (35g) plain flour

1/4 cup (35g) self-raising flour

Beat eggs in small bowl with electric mixer until thick and creamy (this will take about 8 minutes). Add the sugar, 1 tablespoon at a time, beating after each addition, until sugar is dissolved; transfer mixture to a large bowl. Sift the dry ingredients together 3 times then sift over egg mixture; fold in gently. Spread into prepared pan. Bake in moderate oven until cake is cooked when tested. Turn out immediately onto wire rack to cool.

Wheat-Free Sponge
[baked in a 20cm x 30cm lamington pan]

This is a gluten-free cake, perfect for people who suffer from coeliac disease and do not tolerate wheat flour. Cornflour, also called cornstarch in some countries, is made from corn kernels and contains no gluten. Use care when purchasing cornflour because there is a wheaten cornflour available which, as its name suggests, contains wheat.

3 eggs

1/2 cup (110g) caster sugar

3/4 cup (105g) cornflour

Beat eggs in small bowl with electric mixer until thick and creamy (this will take about 8 minutes). Add the sugar, 1 tablespoon at a time, beating after each addition. Sift cornflour 3 times then sift over egg mixture, fold in gently. Spread into prepared pan. Bake in moderate oven until cake is cooked when tested. Turn out immediately onto wire rack to cool.

COOKING TIME CHART

Most of the pans used in this book are available from any department store. The special shaped pans, such as the oval or the Dolly Varden mould, are available from cake-decorating suppliers and specialty cookware stores. You may be able to hire some of the more unusual size pans from specialist cake shops or suppliers.

TYPE OF CAKE PAN	NUMBER OF PACKET CAKES	COOKING TIME	TYPE OF CAKE PAN	NUMBER OF PACKET CAKES	COOKING TIME
Deep 17cm Round	1 packet	1 hour	12-Hole Muffin Pan (1/3-cup/80ml capacity)	1 packet	15 minutes
Deep 20cm Round	1 packet	50 minutes			
	1½ packets	1 hour	20cm x 30cm Lamington Pan	1 packet	25 minutes
Deep 22cm Round	1 packet	40 minutes		1½ packets	40 minutes
	1½ packets	1 hour	20cm Dolly Varden Mould (2.5-litre/10-cup capacity)	1½ packets	1¼ hours
Deep 25cm Round	2 packets	1 hour			
Deep 28cm Round	3 packets	1½ hours	22cm Savarin Pan	½ packet	20 minutes
Deep 30cm Round	3 packets	1¼ hours	7cm deep x 30.5cm Heart-Shaped Pan	3 packets	1¼ hours
31cm Oval	3 packets	1½ hours			
Deep 19cm Square	1½ packets	1 hour	2.25-litre (9-cup) Pudding Steamer	1½ packets	1 hour
Deep 23cm Square	2 packets	1 hour			
23cm Square Slab	1 packet	35 minutes	26cm x 32cm Baking Dish (base measurements)	2 packets	35 minutes
				3 packets	45 minutes
Deep 30cm Square	3 packets	1½ hours	26cm x 36cm Baking Dish (base measurements)	3 packets	1 hour
	4 packets	1¾ hours			

All cooking times are based on a 340g packet of White Wings Golden Buttercake Cake Mix baked in a moderate oven (180°C).

Preparation, Techniques and Clever Decorating Tips

The Fantastic Cakes in this book were made from 340g packets of White Wings Golden Buttercake Cake Mix. The patterns that have been supplied for those fantastic cakes requiring them are of actual size.

GREASING AND LINING THE CAKE PAN

All cake pans, moulds, etc, were greased lightly but evenly with a pastry brush dipped in a little melted butter. An alternative method is to spray pans with cooking-oil spray. We lined the bases of the pans used with baking paper.

To fit baking paper, place your chosen pan, right-side up, on a piece of baking paper then trace around the base with a pencil. Cut out the paper shape just slightly inside the marked area, to allow for the thickness of the pan.

BOWL SIZES

Below are the different sized bowls called for in this book: we recommend you use the exact size specified when combining, beating, etc, cake ingredients. The large bowl's capacity is 15 cups (3.75 litres), the medium holds 11 cups (2.75 litres) and the small holds 7 cups (1.75 litres).

MAKING THE CAKE

For best results: use an electric mixer when beating the cake mixture; follow the directions on the packet; and have all ingredients at room temperature. A large mixing bowl has the capacity to hold up to 4 packet mixes. It's best to mix single packets in a small bowl, and 2 or more packets in either a medium or large bowl.

BAKING THE CAKE

The important thing to remember when baking the cakes is that the pans do not touch one another, the sides of the oven or the door. Whether you are baking cakes on the same shelf or on different shelves, rearrange their positions about halfway during cooking time. When a small cake is baked with a larger one (which will take longer to bake), position the smaller one toward the front of the oven initially, then move the larger cake to that position to complete their baking time. When 2 or more cakes are being baked in an oven at the same time, baking time may be slightly longer than specified. If your cake starts to brown too much, cover it loosely with foil.

TESTING THE CAKE

Ovens vary so much that cooking times should be taken as a guide only: start checking cakes about 5 to 10 minutes before our recommended time. When cooked properly, a cake should shrink slightly from the side of the pan, and the top should feel firm but spring back when pressed lightly with your finger. If in doubt, test by inserting a skewer into the centre of the cake; if any mixture clings to the skewer the cake needs a little more baking. Do not insert the skewer into a crack; this results in an inaccurate reading.

LARGE · MEDIUM · SMALL

SWEETS AND DECORATIONS

We used a large variety of readily available sweets and other decorations on our cakes. Some of those sweets that are known by different names in different areas or are more obscure have been pictured with the appropriate recipe; several are defined in the Glossary on page 117. Non-edible decorations were purchased from toy shops, supermarkets, department stores and craft shops. When placing trimming, such as lace, braid, ribbon, etc, on a frosted cake (as shown at left), back it with sticky tape and position it on the cake at the last minute because the butter from the frosting will discolour the fabric.

PREPARING THE CAKE FOR DECORATING

Some cake mixtures may rise unevenly or peak; if this happens, the top will have to be levelled with a serrated knife. To avoid cake crumbs sticking to the frosting, bake the cake the day before you intend to decorate it. After the cake cools, store it in an airtight container or wrap it securely in plastic wrap. Many cakes in this book used the smooth base as the top of the finished cake, so it's a good idea to cool cakes upside down.

For round boards, snip paper at intervals, as shown, then fold over and tape securely to the underside of the board, neatening with a paper circle glued in position.

Position cake on the prepared board; secure pattern on top of cake with toothpicks then, using the pattern as a guide, use a skewer or toothpick to pierce pattern to transfer markings onto cakes. Cut the cake shape using a small pointed knife.

PREPARING CAKE BOARDS

To make the cake easy to handle as well as more attractive, place it on a board that has been covered with decorative paper. We've given an approximate cake-board size with each recipe. Using Masonite or a similarly strong board, cut your selected paper 5cm to 10cm larger than the shaped board.

To cover square or rectangular boards, fold paper neatly at the corners and tape securely to the underside of the board.

Complete the back with another square of paper glued into position to cover turned-over edges of the top piece.

FOOD COLOURINGS

We used high-quality edible liquid, paste and powdered colourings, most of which are available from cake-decorating suppliers and some health food stores. For bold, strong colours such as reds and blacks, paste and powdered colourings will give you the best results. It's best to dip a toothpick or skewer into a liquid colouring then adding it, in minuscule amounts, to the frosting until the desired colour is reached. Use care when handling food colourings as they stain. Coloured frosting can become darker or lighter on standing, so keep this in mind when decorating a cake ahead of time.

COLOURING SUGAR CRYSTALS

Throughout this book, we used Cake Mate coloured sugar crystals, but it is easy to make your own.

Place sugar in a plastic bag; add a drop or two of liquid colouring and work it into the sugar by shaking and pressing the closed bag. This method works well for colouring coconut and dried pasta too.

FROSTING

This is a good basic frosting recipe. You can vary the flavour by adding a few drops of an essence, or a little finely grated orange, lemon or lime rind.

Here are two points to remember when making the frosting:
• Don't overbeat the butter.
• If colouring frosting, slightly decrease the amount of milk used; otherwise, the frosting could curdle. If it does curdle, just beat in a little extra icing sugar.

125g soft butter

1½ cups (240g) icing sugar mixture

2 tablespoons milk, approximately

Beat butter in small bowl with electric mixer until light in colour, gradually beat in half the icing sugar, then the milk, then the remaining icing sugar. Flavour and colour as desired.

Chocolate Frosting Sift ⅓ cup (35g) cocoa powder with the icing sugar.

PIPING BAGS

We have used piping bags throughout this book. You can purchase a ready-made bag, or make your own using greaseproof or baking paper, or a small plastic bag.

Making a paper piping bag

Cut a 30cm square of non-stick baking or greaseproof paper in half diagonally; twist into a cone shape. Staple or fold the cone to hold its shape.

Half fill cone with frosting, cream or cooled melted chocolate, then fold the top edges of the cone over on themselves to keep frosting or chocolate contained. Hold bag closed securely when piping, as shown, squeezing gently but firmly.

Making a plastic piping bag

Spoon frosting or chocolate into a small plastic bag, easing contents down into a corner; twist top of bag to secure. Snip a tiny bit off the corner of the bag to pipe.

Fluffing

Corrugating

Marbling

Glossary

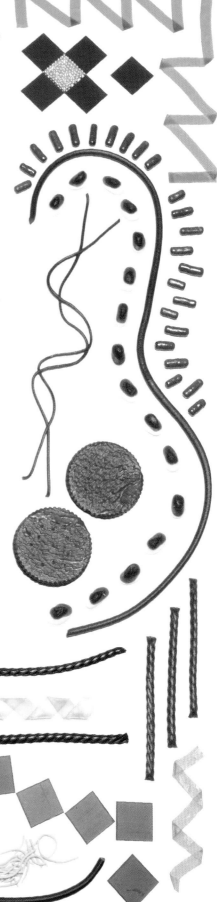

CACHOUS also known as dragées; tiny hard sugar balls, available in silver, gold or various colours

CHANG'S FRIED NOODLES ready-to-serve egg noodles pre-fried in vegetable oil

CHOCOLATE BULLETS also known as LICORICE ROCKETS small chocolate-coated cylinders of licorice

CHOCOLATE MONTES chocolate-coated oval-shaped plain sugar biscuit (cookie)

CHOC THINS: tradename for packaged flaked cocoa-flavoured sprinkles

COCONUT

Desiccated unsweetened, dried, finely grated coconut

Shredded thin strips of unsweetened dried coconut flesh

Toasted place desiccated or shredded coconut either in a heavy-base pan on top of the stove or on an oven tray inside a moderate oven, stirring occasionally, until browned lightly

COLOURINGS there are wide variations in the quality and density of the various colourings available, so it's always best to tint a small sample of what you intend to colour, then cover and allow it to stand for several hours. With time, some colours will intensify while others fade. Liquid, pastes and gel colourings can be used straight from their containers, which are best kept in a cup while being used in case of spills

DOLLY VARDEN MOULD spherical, bombe-shaped mould that can be used for baking as well as for making frozen or chilled dishes

DRIED CURRANT a tiny black raisin sometimes referred to just as "currant"

FAIRY FLOSS also known as cotton candy; a fluffy confection made from spun-sugar, often tinted pink

FLAKE crunchy chocolate-bar confection so fragile it "flakes"

FRUIT ROLL-UPS – METRES tradename of rolled strips of various kinds of real fruit paste rolled flat into metre lengths

JERSEY football sweater, pullover, Guernsey

LAMINGTON PAN a shallow (2.5cm deep) 20cm x 30cm rectangular pan used for baking cakes – traditionally, a coconut- and chocolate-covered sponge

LICORICE

Straps 2.5cm-wide, metre-long flat "tyre-tread" strips of black licorice

Super Ropes 85cm-long round pieces of red or black licorice

Thin Red Rope same length and diameter as cooked spaghetti

Twists short twisted round pieces of red or black licorice

PAVLOVA SHELLS ready-made packaged meringue shells, commonly sold singly in a large 30cm round

RAINBOW FRUIT ROLL-UPS tradename of rolled multi-coloured strips of various kinds of real fruit paste rolled flat into individual squares

READY-MADE ICING commercially made packaged fondant icing ready to be tinted and rolled out to cover a cake

ROCKY ROAD a chunky confection traditionally made from milk chocolate-covered peanuts, marshmallows, coconut and, occasionally, glace cherries

SAVARIN PAN a heatproof ring mould named after the baba-like, rum-soaked rich yeast cake for which it was designed; its use has been extended to include many other cakes and uncooked recipes such as moulded jelly

STRAWBERRIES & CREAM a commercially made pecan-sized, creamy-based confection having a strawberry-flavoured topping

SWISS THINS: commercially packaged delicate extra-fine 4cm-squares of Swiss milk chocolate

WAGON WHEEL packaged chocolate-coated biscuit (cookie) marshmallow- and jam-filled snack

Index

FACTS AND FIGURES

Wherever you live, you'll be able to use our recipes with the help of these easy-to-follow conversions. While these conversions are approximate only, the difference between an exact and the approximate conversion of various liquid and dry measures is but minimal and will not affect your cooking results.

DRY MEASURES

Metric	Imperial
15g	1/2oz
30g	1oz
60g	2oz
90g	3oz
125g	4oz (1/4lb)
155g	5oz
185g	6oz
220g	7oz
250g	8oz (1/2lb)
280g	9oz
315g	10oz
345g	11oz
375g	12oz (3/4lb)
410g	13oz
440g	14oz
470g	15oz
500g	16oz (1lb)
750g	24oz (1 1/2lb)
1kg	32oz (2lb)

LIQUID MEASURES

Metric	Imperial
30ml	1 fluid oz
60ml	2 fluid oz
100ml	3 fluid oz
125ml	4 fluid oz
150ml	5 fluid oz (1/4 pint/1 gill)
190ml	6 fluid oz
250ml	8 fluid oz
300ml	10 fluid oz (1/2 pint)
500ml	16 fluid oz
600ml	20 fluid oz (1 pint)
1000ml (1 litre)	1 3/4 pints

HELPFUL MEASURES

Metric	Imperial
3mm	1/8in
6mm	1/4in
1cm	1/2in
2cm	3/4in
2.5cm	1in
5cm	2in
6cm	2 1/2in
8cm	3in
10cm	4in
13cm	5in
15cm	6in
18cm	7in
20cm	8in
23cm	9in
25cm	10in
28cm	11in
30cm	12in (1ft)

MEASURING EQUIPMENT

The difference between one country's measuring cups and another's is, at most, within a 2 or 3 teaspoon variance. (For the record, 1 Australian metric measuring cup holds approximately 250ml.) The most accurate way of measuring dry ingredients is to weigh them. When measuring liquids, use a clear glass or plastic jug with the metric markings.

If you would like to purchase The Australian Women's Weekly Test Kitchen's metric measuring cups and spoons (as approved by Standards Australia), turn to page 120 for details and order coupon. You will receive:

- a graduated set of 4 cups for measuring dry ingredients, with sizes marked on the cups.
- a graduated set of 4 spoons for measuring dry and liquid ingredients, with amounts marked on the spoons.
- 1 teaspoon: 5ml.
- 1 tablespoon: 20ml.

Note: North America and UK use 15ml tablespoons. All cup and spoon measurements are level.

How To Measure

When using graduated metric measuring cups, shake dry ingredients loosely into the appropriate cup. Do not tap the cup on a bench or tightly pack the ingredients unless directed to do so. Level top of measuring cups and measuring spoons with a knife. When measuring liquids, place a clear glass or plastic jug with metric markings on a flat surface to check accuracy at eye level.

We use large eggs having an average weight of 60g.

OVEN TEMPERATURES

These oven temperatures are only a guide. Always check the manufacturer's manual.

	C° (Celsius)	F° (Fahrenheit)	Gas Mark
Very slow	120	250	1
Slow	150	300	2
Moderately slow	160	325	3
Moderate	180 - 190	350 - 375	4
Moderately hot	200 - 210	400 - 425	5
Hot	220 - 230	450 - 475	6
Very hot	240 - 250	500 - 525	7

Looking after your interest...

Keep your Home Library cookbooks clean, tidy and within easy reach with slipcovers designed to hold up to 12 books. *Plus* you can follow our recipes perfectly with a set of accurate measuring cups and spoons, as used by *The Australian Women's Weekly* Test Kitchen.

TO ORDER

Mail or fax Photocopy or complete the coupon below and post to AWW Home Library Reader Offer, ACP Direct, PO Box 7036, Sydney NSW 1028, *or* fax to (02) 9267 4363.

Credit cards Have your details ready then, if you live in Sydney, phone 9260 0000; if you live elsewhere in Australia, phone 1800 252 515 (free call, Mon-Fri, 8.30am-5.30pm).

PRICE

Book Holder $11.95 (Australia); elsewhere $A21.95.

Metric Measuring Set $5.95 (Australia); $A8.00 (New Zealand); $A9.95 elsewhere. Prices include postage and handling. This offer is available in all countries.

PAYMENT

Australian residents We accept the credit cards listed on the coupon, money orders and cheques.

Overseas residents We accept the credit cards listed on the coupon, drafts in $A drawn on an Australian bank, and also British, New Zealand and U.S. cheques in the currency of the country of issue. Credit card charges are at the exchange rate current at the time of payment.
